THE **WHARNCLIFFE COMPANION** TO

MANCHESTER

Town Hall, Manchester.

THE **WHARNCLIFFE COMPANION** TO

MANCHESTER

AN **A** TO **Z** OF LOCAL HISTORY

GLYNIS COOPER

Wharncliffe Books

First published in Great Britain in 2005 by
Wharncliffe Books
an imprint of
Pen & Sword Books Ltd
47 Church Street
Barnsley
South Yorkshire
S70 2AS

ISBN 1-903425-74-3

A CIP catalogue record for this book is
available from the British Library

Typeset in 10/11.5pt Plantin by Mac Style Ltd, Scarborough, N. Yorkshire
Printed and bound in England by CPI UK

Pen & Sword Books Ltd incorporates the Imprints of Pen & Sword Aviation,
Pen & Sword Maritime, Pen & Sword Military, Wharncliffe Local History,
Pen & Sword Select, Pen and Sword Military Classics and Leo Cooper.

For a complete list of Wharncliffe titles, please contact
Wharncliffe Books Limited
47 Church Street, Barnsley, South Yorkshire, S70 2AS, England
E-mail: enquiries@pen-and-sword.co.uk
Website: www.wharncliffebooks.co.uk

Contents

Extensions of Manchester since 1838.

Preface and Acknowledgements

To produce a complete historical encyclopedia of Manchester: the city, its history, its culture, its industry, its traditions and its achievements; would fill a dozen volumes. Here it has been decided mostly to exclude the Greater Manchester area, which includes Trafford, Salford, Wigan, Bolton, Bury, Rochdale, Oldham, Tameside and Stockport, and to concentrate on the city itself and the surrounding suburbs. However it is unavoidable that there will be overlaps and omissions and for these the writer apologises to her readers.

Compiling a one-volume encyclopedia of even this limited area is a highly selective task which focuses on just some of the thousands of places and events, the millions of people and their achievements, which have made Manchester the city it is today. Many assumed that with the decline of the cotton industry Manchester's days as a great city were over. Nothing could be further from the truth. The city has fought its way back from the brink of the abyss to become a national and international centre for art, culture, sport, technology, education and tourism. Manchester has given a new meaning to the word 'regeneration' and has now overtaken Birmingham to become the second city of England. Some would even say the first.

The scope of this encyclopedia is as wide ranging as possible within its limitations and covers places, people, events, the development of the city, history and archaeology, mills, warehouses, churches, inns, civic buildings, health, education, sport, transport, retail and businesses, legends, old customs, the media, and a score of other details which go to make up Manchester from its beginnings to the 21st century. Hopefully the book will prove an interesting companion for both those who know the city well and for those who are just passing through; and it is hoped that it will give readers some idea of Manchester's past and how it has shaped Manchester's present.

For more detailed information on subjects, websites and books for further reading are listed. The Central Library and the Tourist Information Centre, both situated on St Peter's Square, are invaluable sources of information. The author hopes that the chosen selections will prove interesting and informative, offering starting points for those who want to know more.

I would like to thank the staff of Manchester Central Library and the editorial team at Wharncliffe Books.

For Michael Wood, a fellow Mancunian and historian, who has never forgotten his Manchester roots either.

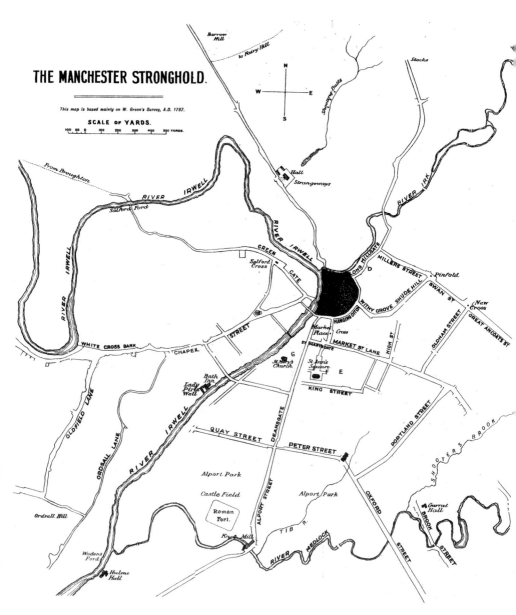

The Manchester stronghold: Manchester in 1787 before the cotton mills (Lancs and Cheshire Historical Society, 1904)

The Wharncliffe Companion to Manchester

A

ADULT DEAF AND DUMB INSTITUTE
Govesnor St, All Saints (off Oxford Rd). This was established in 1850.
Children's facilities had existed since 1823.
GLYNIS COOPER, *THE ILLUSTRATED HISTORY OF THE MANCHESTER SUBURBS*
(2002).

AFFLECKS PALACE
On the corner of Church St and Tib St. 'An independent enterprise for the
independent entrepreneur' is how Afflecks describes itself. Behind its Art

Afflecks Palace on Tib St.

Deco façade and a notice which states 'and on the seventh day God created MANchester', there are four floors of alternative and individual clothes shops, jewellery, music and offbeat shops, with a wholefood cafe on the top floor offering cheap tasty food and excellent cappuccino. There are no lifts or escalators and the stairs are steep and narrow but the place offers an experience out of the ordinary.
WWW.AFFLECKS-PALACE.CO.UK

AGRICOLA (AD 37–93)

Roman statesman, soldier and Governor of Britain 77–87, he built the first Roman fort at Castlefield, and his statue stands in a niche on the Town Hall in Albert Square.
CHAMBERS BIOGRAPHICAL DICTIONARY.

AHERNE, CAROLINE (B. 1963)

Caroline Aherne was born in Wythenshawe, the daughter of an Irish railway worker, and attended the Hollies Convent Grammar School in West Didsbury before studying drama at Liverpool Polytechnic. A comedienne, she created the character of Mrs Merton but is best known for her role as the lazy daughter in *The Royle Family*.
WWW.MANCHESTER2002-UK.COM

AINSWORTH, WILLIAM HARRISON (1805–1882)

Ainsworth was born in King St and educated at Manchester Grammar School. He was articled to a law firm but became a prolific romantic novelist instead. He married Fanny Ebers whose father was a publisher. Among his many novels were *Rookwood*, *The Lancashire Witches*, *The Manchester Rebels* and *Guy Fawkes*, which is set in Ordsall Hall, Salford, where Fawkes is supposed to have hatched the Gunpowder Plot.
☛ *See also Ordsall Hall; Guy Fawkes and The Seven Stars.*
WWW.MANCHESTER2002-UK.COM

ALBERT MEMORIAL MONUMENT

Albert Square. An ornate monument, reflecting the interests of Prince Albert and the contributions he made to English life, designed by Thomas Worthington and erected in 1862 on Albert Square in the wake of the tragedy of his untimely death from typhoid which marked a ten year period of mourning for his widow, Queen Victoria.
WWW.MANCHESTER2002-UK.COM

ALL SAINTS CHURCH

Chorlton-on-Medlock. All Saints Church stood opposite Grosvenor Place on Oxford Rd. It did not seem to be a lucky church. Built in 1820, it was partially destroyed by fire in 1850 shortly before a wedding was due to take place there, and restored, only to be blitzed in 1940 and demolished in 1945. The site and the former graveyard are now a pleasant recreational park which borders the All Saints building and the library of Manchester Metropolitan University. All Saints drinking fountain, a splendidly ornate and overfussy Victorian creation, was erected in 1896 just outside the gates of All Saints Church and remained there until 1982.

GLYNIS COOPER, *THE HISTORY OF THE MANCHESTER SUBURBS* (2002).

ANCOATS

Derives its name from 'ana cots', which means lonely cottages. This tiny hamlet became the world's first industrial suburb and through modern regeneration turning the wheel full circle is now set to become the world's first urban village. Ancoats was a densely packed millscape suburb which included McConnell and Kennedy's steam-driven mill built in 1794; Murray Mill, also steam-driven, built in 1798; Jersey Mill, Beehive Mill and Pin Mill. Rows of cramped little 'back-to-back' workers cottages surrounded the mills. It is said that the sun never shone properly through the smoke of the mills and cottages of Ancoats. Many of the old mills have survived and are now Grade II listed buildings. Today Ancoats has a cosmopolitan population of Irish, Polish and Italian communities. The area has been immortalized by Howard Spring in his novels *Fame is the Spur* and *My Son, My Son* and by Mrs Linnaeus Banks in *The Manchester Man*.

☛ *See also ANCOATS HALL.*

GLYNIS COOPER, *THE ILLUSTRATED HISTORY OF THE MANCHESTER SUBURBS* (2002).

ANCOATS HALL

The Old Hall was a black and white timbered moated grange which stood on the corner of Every St. It was demolished by mill owner George Murray in 1829. The New Hall also stood on Every St but by 1900 it had become part of Manchester Art Museum. It was known as the Horsfall Museum and was reported to have haunted vaults. It has not survived.

GLYNIS COOPER, *THE ILLUSTRATED HISTORY OF THE MANCHESTER SUBURBS* (2002).

ANCOATS INDUSTRIAL ARCHAEOLOGY

Ancoats took the brunt of the first enthusiastic flurry of mill building in the 1790s until the industry was so intense that Alexis de Tocqueville could write

> thick black smoke covers the city ... the sun appears like a disc without any rays ... in this semi-daylight 300,000 people work ceaselessly.

In 1845 Friedrich Engels added:

> included under the name Ancoats stand the largest mills of Manchester lining the canals, colossal six and seven storied buildings towering with their slender chimneys far above the low cottages of the workers ...

Today in Ancoats, as elsewhere, the Age of Cotton is long since over and many of the mills have gone. During the latter part of the 20th century, with heritage taking a high profile, it was decided that, in the interests of industrial archaeology and posterity, what remained of the Ancoats millscapes should be preserved. Surveys and restoration work are being carried out as part of the East Manchester regeneration scheme and serious attempts are being made to utilize the old buildings so that they become part of 21st-century life. Clubs, recording studios and countless musicians have discovered the excellent acoustic properties of the old mills. The Murray Brothers' 'court of mills with its grand gateway and Rochdale Canal basin' is being restored so that an understanding of the millscapes will be provided for future generations. Some of the mills are being refurbished to offer luxury living quarters in the heart of the city; a purpose our 19th-century forebears would perhaps have found ironic.

☛ *See also* ANCOATS.

WWW.GMAU.ORG/; WWW.ART.MAN.AC.UK/FIELDARCHAEOLOGYCENTRE/

ANGLO-SAXON MANCHESTER

Mamceastre, as Manchester was originally known, was first attacked by Saxon warriors in AD 429; and again in 620 by an invasion from the north-east kingdom of Deira led by Edwin, king of Northumbria. The major contribution made by the Saxons was to settle most of the townships and villages which would eventually grow and unite to form the modern city of Manchester.

GLYNIS COOPER, *THE ILLUSTRATED HISTORY OF THE MANCHESTER SUBURBS* (2002).

ARCHIMEDES

Granby Row. A larger than life model of Archimedes sitting in his bath tub stands under a railway arch not far from the Vimto monument, placed there by the University of Manchester Institute of Science and Technology (UMIST). Archimedes (287–212 BC) was a major scholar and perhaps one of the first true mechanics. He was a renowned Greek scientist who specialized in mechanics, hydrostatics and geometry. He proved that 'a body plunged into fluid loses as much of its weight as is equal to the weight of an equal volume of the fluid', which is probably the reason why swimmers feel that their bodies are lighter when they are in the water and why the sculpture

Archimedes rising from his bath tub beneath a railway arch facing UMIST (off Granby Row).

under the arches shows Archimedes rising from his bath tub. Archimedes also invented siege-breaking engines, the 'endless screw' and the 'Archimedes screw' which was a spiral pump for drawing up water.
CHAMBERS BIOGRAPHICAL DICTIONARY.

ARDWICK

This suburb grew from a Saxon farm to a lively Tudor village which had problems with 'wild women, disorderly houses, children playing giddy gaddy and too many dung hills in the road'. Things didn't improve with the coming of the Industrial Revolution and Ardwick must have been a pretty unpleasant place at times with its dye works, chemical works, brick works, boiler works and rubber works in close proximity to the mills.

Ardwick Green was however rather more upmarket and home to John Rylands, a cotton magnate whose fortune founded the John Rylands

University Library; Mrs Linnaeus Banks who wrote *The Manchester Man*; and the parents of Edmund Potter.

The first Ragged School for poor and deprived children was opened in Dark Lane *c*.1852. Next to Hyde Rd Bus Depot (formerly the Tramways Depot) stands the former Ellen Wilkinson School, originally Nicholl's Hospital, a boys' school modelled on Chetham's College and built in 1881. Ellen Wilkinson was born in Ardwick, became an MP in 1924, took part in the Jarrow Hunger March of 1936 and was appointed Minister for Education in the post-war Labour Government. There was also an entertainments complex in Ardwick which included theatres, cinemas, a billiard hall and a wrestling stadium. Today all that remains is the Apollo Theatre.

GLYNIS COOPER, *THE ILLUSTRATED HISTORY OF THE MANCHESTER SUBURBS* (2002); CHRIS MAKEPEACE, *LOOKING BACK AT HULME, MOSS SIDE, CHORLTON-ON-MEDLOCK AND ARDWICK* (1998).

ARNDALE CENTRE
Dominating Market St, part of the former commercial centre of the city, the Arndale was once the largest shopping centre in Europe, and now has over 200 shops including many high street chain stores such as Boots, BHS, Littlewoods, W H Smith, Dixons, Mothercare and Tandy.

WWW.MANCHESTER2002-UK.COM

ARKWRIGHT'S MILL
Shude Hill. Built in 1788 by Richard Arkwright, who was credited with inventing the water frame, this was one of the very earliest cotton mills. It was demolished during the 20th century.

ROBINA MCNEIL AND MICHAEL NEVELL, *A GUIDE TO THE INDUSTRIAL ARCHAEOLOGY OF GREATER MANCHESTER* (2000); MIKE WILLIAMS WITH D A FARNIE, *COTTON MILLS IN GREATER MANCHESTER* (1992).

ASHTON CANAL
In 1796 the Manchester and Ashton Canal was built. It was the first canal to reach the Portland Basin and connected the Bridgewater Canal and Manchester to the Huddersfield Canal. It also connected with the Rochdale Canal in the Piccadilly Basin.

ALAN KIDD, *HISTORY OF MANCHESTER* (3RD EDN, 2002).

ASIA HOUSE
Asia House stands at 82 Princess St and was a textile warehouse. The River Medlock flows around the rear of the building where the entrance to the Duke of Bridgewater's 'lost canal' can still just be seen as a curved arch in the brickwork barely above water level.

SIMON TAYLOR ET AL., *MANCHESTER: THE WAREHOUSE LEGACY* (2002).

ATHERTON, MIKE (B. 1966)

Born in Failsworth, Mike Atherton attended Manchester Grammar School where he was cricket captain for three years. At 16 he captained the England Under-19 cricket team. In the mid-1980s he read history at Cambridge and toured with the England Young Cricketers in Sri Lanka and Australia. Atherton made his debut for Lancashire County Cricket Club in 1987 and won his county cap in 1989. He played his first Test match against Australia at Old Trafford in 1989 and later in New Zealand became the youngest Lancastrian century maker. Atherton was named Wisden cricketer of the year in 1991 and in 1993 he became the England team captain. He made his reputation as a good all-rounder and defensive player. After his hundredth Test appearance (against the West Indies at Old Trafford) in 2000 Atherton announced his retirement from first class cricket.

WWW.MANCHESTER2002-UK.COM

B

BAGULEY HALL, WYTHENSHAWE

Baggiley Manor is mentioned in Domesday Book but the Hall was built *c*.1320 by Sir William de Baggiley who was knighted by Edward I and married one of his illegitimate daughters. Baguley is a name derived from badger clearing. The Hall was a black and white timbered building with fine 14th-century groining and open trefoil work.

Sir William's son and daughter, John and Isabell, were co-heirs to the estate. Isabell married Sir John Legh who was related to the Legh family of Lyme Park near Disley; and the last male descendant of the Baguley Hall Leghs married Elinour, daughter of William Tatton of Wythenshawe. By the 1960s the Hall had become a timber store but it was fully restored in the 1980s by Manchester Corporation and still survives today.

GLYNIS COOPER, *THE ILLUSTRATED HISTORY OF THE MANCHESTER SUBURBS* (2002); JEAN AND SHEILA CLARKE, *WYTHENSHAWE* (1984).

BAMFORD, SAMUEL (1788–1872)

The son of a muslin weaver from Middleton he was educated at Manchester Grammar School. He was one of the speakers at Peterloo and he wrote radical working-class material and poetry. His semi-autobiographical *Passages in the Life of a Radical* (1840–4) gives a valuable insight into the social conditions of the working classes in the first part of the 19th century.

WWW.MANCHESTER2002-UK.COM; WWW.SPINNINGTHEWEB.ORG.UK

BANKS, ISABELLA (1823–1897)

She was born in Oldham and married lecturer and journalist Linnaeus Banks. Mrs Linnaeus Banks (as she preferred to be known) detested the

social and industrial changes of 19th-century Manchester and she wrote *The Manchester Man* which immortalized the unspeakably awful conditions in Ancoats and other millscape suburbs. She also wrote poetry, of which *Ivy Leaves* published in 1843 is her best known work.
WWW.MANCHESTER2002-UK.COM

BARBIROLLI, SIR JOHN (1899–1970)
London-born violin player and cellist and conductor who revitalized the Hallé Orchestra after the Second World War by employing talented musicians and improving wages. Barbirolli transformed the Hallé from a provincial orchestra to one of world-class renown. He succeeded Toscanini as conductor of the New York Philharmonic Orchestra in 1937 but returned to England to become a permanent conductor with the Hallé in 1943. He married Evelyn Rothwell, the oboist with the Hallé, in 1939, and was given the Freedom of Manchester in 1958.
CHAMBERS BIOGRAPHICAL DICTIONARY.

BARONIAL WAREHOUSE
A warehouse at 74 Princess St designed in the Scottish Baronial style in 1880. It looks like a grand Transylvanian castle.
SIMON TAYLOR ET AL., MANCHESTER: THE WAREHOUSE LEGACY (2002).

BBC
Greater Manchester Radio (GMR) 95.1 and 104.6 FM operates from the television building on Oxford Rd and broadcasts news, music, sport and general talk radio. BBC Television is situated on Oxford Rd close to the River

BBC, Oxford Rd.

Medlock and produces local news (*Look North West*) and community programmes; sport; Asian programmes; *Songs of Praise*, etc. WWW.BBC.CO.UK

BEACONS FOR A BRIGHTER FUTURE

Regeneration work in Clayton, Beswick, Bradford, which built the Games stadium and velodrome.

ALAN KIDD, *HISTORY OF MANCHESTER* (3RD EDN, 2002); WWW.MANCHESTER 2002-UK.COM

BECKHAM, DAVID (B. 1975)

Born in Leytonstone, Beckham won the Bobby Charlton Soccer Skills Award when he was 12 and signed as a trainee for Manchester United in 1991. He was named Carling Player of the Month in August 1996; Sky Sports Fans Footballer in 1996; PFA Young Player of the Year in 1997 and Sir Matt Busby Player of the Year in 1997. His marriage to 'Posh Spice', member of an all-girl singing group, has given him a high 'showbiz' profile and he is rarely out of the tabloids. Beckham transferred to Real Madrid in 2003.

WWW.MANCHESTER2002-UK.COM

BEEHIVE MILL

Jersey St, Ancoats. L-shaped five-storey cotton mill built in 1824, it had thirteen bays on Radium St and three on Jersey St. This mill is an early example of fireproof construction. It was extended in 1850. It still exists and is used as music and recording studios.

ROBINA MCNEIL AND MICHAEL NEVELL, *A GUIDE TO THE INDUSTRIAL ARCHAEOLOGY OF GREATER MANCHESTER* (2000); MIKE WILLIAMS WITH D A FARNIE, *COTTON MILLS IN GREATER MANCHESTER* (1992).

BELLE VUE

In 1836 Belle Vue Tea Gardens were established on Hyde Rd and in 1843 John Jennison expanded the gardens by 13 acres, adding a lake and a natural history museum. This was followed in 1847 by a maze in the gardens and a greyhound track near the Longsight entrance. Three years later a two-storey building was constructed by this entrance which housed a ballroom for 500 people. Over the next half-century monkeys, camels, bears, lions, elephants and a sea-lion pool were added to the existing gardens, and Italian Gardens, a new maze, an Indian Grotto and a fireworks stand were built, plus a ballroom which would hold 10,000 people. In the 20th century there was a funfair, roller skating, a scenic railway and a miniature railway, speedway, stockcar racing, a 32-lane bowling alley and regular concerts were given by the Hallé Orchestra. Belle Vue offered so much but times and tastes change and on 30 January 1982 the gates closed for the last time. There is still a greyhound track and a multiscreen Showcase Cinema has been built adjacent to it, along with a neighbouring pizza restaurant which has a double-locking entry system for security; but even the name Belle Vue has now been erased from the station board at Ashburys railway station.

The John Rylands Library on Deansgate holds the Belle Vue archive and ephemera such as programmes for the shows and events which took place there. During the late 1880s Buffalo Bill (Bill Cody) toured the North-West with a Wild West Show which included real Indian chiefs and braves. Buffalo Bill returned with them in 1903 and there is an old photograph of him with his Indian chiefs and braves in full Red Indian war costume and feathered headdresses on a tram near Hyde Rd, looking for all the world as though they are on a day trip to Blackpool.

GLYNIS COOPER, *ILLUSTRATED HISTORY OF THE MANCHESTER SUBURBS* (2002).

BEST, GEORGE (B. 1946)

Born in Northern Ireland, Best made a name for himself playing for Manchester United 1963–74. He played a forward position and was voted Footballer of the Year in 1968. He made 466 appearances for Manchester United and scored 178 goals. Although his football skills were not in doubt, he was a 'flawed genius' which led to his early retirement from the game.

WWW.MANCHESTER2002-UK.COM

BESWICK

This is one of the smaller of the Manchester suburbs which has lost much of its individual identity in recent times and is often bracketed with its much larger neighbour of Clayton. Beswick is centred around Grey Mare Lane and Ashton Old and New Roads. It is a typical rather drab millscape suburb which is now beginning to benefit from the East Manchester Regeneration Scheme. Beswick's main claims to fame seem to have been a visit by Buffalo Bill Cody with a tramload of Indian chiefs and braves in 1903 and the fact that CWS Bakeries were based there.

GLYNIS COOPER, *THE ILLUSTRATED HISTORY OF THE MANCHESTER SUBURBS* (2002).

BIRCH HALL, RUSHOLME

The earliest deeds for the estate dated back to 1190, which included woods for grazing swine and a corn mill, though Birch Hall, the seat of the Birch family, was built sometime during the 16th century. The Hall was a fine black and white timbered house which stood on the site of earlier building. Birch Fold Cottage (demolished in 1912), a black and white timbered, thatched cottage, once moated, which stood nearby, may have predated the Hall.

Oliver Cromwell is said to have slept here during one of the Civil War campaigns. Birch Hall Farm, the home farm to the Hall, also stood close by. Additions to Birch Hall in the 18th and 19th centuries almost obliterated the old black and white manor house. In 1931 the Hall was sold to Manchester Grammar School and demolished to make way for new school buildings. GLYNIS COOPER, *THE ILLUSTRATED HISTORY OF THE MANCHESTER SUBURBS* (2002); PETER HELM AND GAY SUSSEX, *LOOKING BACK AT RUSHOLME AND FALLOWFIELD* (1984).

BLACKLEY

The name means 'clearing in a dark wood' and this is in keeping with stories of mischief associated with Boggart Hole Clough and legends of a haunting by a murder victim in the old Tudor hall in Blackley (demolished 1815). Blackley lies at the northern extremity of the Manchester suburbs and was too far out to have been touched by the millscapes. Although there was an element of the traditional dyeing and bleaching industries, the whole area remained semi rural until at least the 1930s. Booth Hall Children's Hospital, one of the few dedicated children's hospitals in England, lies opposite Boggart Hole Clough. Modern development has not been kind to Blackley, though Heaton Hall Park on the outskirts has retained its charm and character.

☞ *See also HEATON HALL; HEATON PARK; BOGGART HOLE CLOUGH.*
GLYNIS COOPER, *THE ILLUSTRATED HISTORY OF THE MANCHESTER SUBURBS* (2002).

BLITZ, SECOND WORLD WAR

Manchester was badly bombed many times by the Luftwaffe. The worst occasion was just before Christmas in 1940 when 700 people were killed and 2,500 were injured. The Cathedral took a direct hit while the Free Trade Hall and the Royal Exchange were badly damaged, along with 100,000 homes. In other raids All Saints Church on Oxford Rd was partially destroyed and Burnage High School, which had just been rebuilt, was demolished. Firewatchers undertook regular shift rotas on the roofs of higher buildings, searching the skies for approaching planes and falling bombs so that they could give advance warning of approaching fires to try and limit casualties and property damage.
WWW.MANCHESTERONLINE.CO.UK

BOARDMAN, CHRIS (B. 1968)

Although born on the Wirral, Boardman joined the Manchester Wheelers Cycle Club as a junior and helped them to win twenty team and national titles over five years. In 1991 he became British Champion in the 25 mile, 50

mile and pursuit events. He took part in the 1992 Olympics at Barcelona and he won the 4000m individual pursuit event, the World Championship and the Gold Medal. Boardman also became a world record holder in the 4000m and 5000m events and was awarded the CBE in 1993.
WWW.MANCHESTER2002-UK.COM

BOGGART HOLE CLOUGH

Blackley. This quaintly named and lesser known park, close to Heaton Park, has long been known as a natural beauty spot with picturesque landscapes, woods and water. The wooded clough takes its name from a boggart, a mischievous elf which, it is said, had made the quiet wooded clough its home. This particular boggart made itself a nuisance to a family who lived on a farm at White Moss near the head of the clough. It was described as 'an unquiet spirit that manifested itself in a small shrill voice like a baby's penny trumpet'. The boggart didn't do any real harm until one of the sons of the house started to poke fun at it. The boggart took great offence and started inflicting injuries on the farmer's children. When it tried to suffocate one of the children in bed

Waterfall, Boggart Hall Clough, 1905, where the boggart frolicked.

the farmer had had enough. He packed up his family and possessions and moved to new premises.

The boggart was also credited with special powers. If young men could find 'three grains of St John's fernseed in which the boggart had frolicked' then they were assured of winning the love of their sweetheart. A 19th-century writer wrote

> tread softly ... for this Boggart Clough, and see in yonder dark corners, and beneath projecting mossy stones, where the dusky sullen cave yawns before you ... there lurks a strange elf, the sly and mischievous boggart ...

Although the clough is still wooded, it is now many years since the boggart was seen or heard; unable to cope, perhaps, with technological progress and a less romantic, more sceptical approach to life.

HILDA M. MCGILL, *HISTORY OF BLACKLEY* (1939); GLYNIS COOPER, *HIDDEN MANCHESTER* (2004) AND *THE ILLUSTRATED HISTORY OF THE MANCHESTER SUBURBS* (2002); WWW.MANCHESTER2003-UK.COM

BOLTON AND BURY CANAL

Work began on the Bolton and Bury Canal in 1791 which ran from Salford through Manchester to Prestolee between Kearsley and Little Lever, from where one arm ran to Bolton and another to Bury. The canal was 15 miles long and had seventeen locks.

Carriage by canal was slow and gradually the canals lost out to the railways and improved road transport methods. Much of the canal system was gradually allowed to silt up and was lost. In the late 20th century, however, several canal restoration schemes were instigated and the laidback appeal of a narrow-boat holiday has grown dramatically.

G ASHWORTH, *THE LOST RIVERS OF MANCHESTER* (1987); WWW.SPINNINGTHE WEB.ORG.UK

BOMB, IRA

On Father's Day, Saturday 15 June 1996, a 3000lb bomb, planted by the IRA in a Ford van outside Marks and Spencer's, exploded and caused massive damage to surrounding properties. Marks and Spencer's store was completely destroyed. The Royal Exchange and the Old Wellington Inn withstood the blast but windows were shattered and the infrastructure shaken. Miraculously, no one was killed and most of the 206 injuries were relatively minor. Extensive rebuilding and refurbishment has taken place and Manchester city centre has been reinvented. It could be said, with hindsight and in view of the light casualties, that the bomb was the best thing that could

have happened to Manchester, as it necessitated and enabled much needed regeneration of the city centre.
WWW.MANCHESTER2002-UK.COM

BRADFORD
Taking its name from 'Broad Ford', probably from a lost crossing of the River Medlock, Bradford had two distinctive features. Bradford Colliery began production in the 1790s and was active for nearly 200 years. The pithead was finally demolished in 1973. After Bradford's incorporation with Manchester in 1885, the pit was not only close to the city centre, it was within the municipal boundaries. Mills, manufactories, trains and people all needed coal and for those reasons Bradford was an important pit. The other distinction was Philips Park, which opened in 1846 and was named after Mark Philips, one of Manchester's first two MPs after the 1832 Reform Act. With Queens Park it was one of Manchester's first two public parks.
☛ *See also PHILIP'S PARK.*
GLYNIS COOPER, *THE ILLUSTRATED HISTORY OF THE MANCHESTER SUBURBS* (2002).

BRIDGEWATER HALL
Lower Mosley St. This international concert hall, built almost opposite the old Central Station which is now better known as the GMEX, was designed by Renton Howard Wood Levin in 1996, and 'is now one of the most acoustically superior classical music venues in the world'. The Bridgewater Hall (named after the Duke of Bridgewater who pioneered the canal system of transport for cargoes through Manchester in the 18th century) looks down on the Rochdale Canal basin and the narrow-boats moored there; an echo from an earlier age. The auditorium can seat 2,400 people and

> is designed to be warm and dynamic with acoustics carefully designed to produce high quality sound reproduction ... the whole building is mounted on a system of 270 giant foundation 'springs' which isolate it from vibration and resultant noise so that concert-goers can appreciate musical performance without interference ...

The Bridgewater Hall hosts performances by the BBC Philharmonic Orchestra, the Manchester Camerata and other leading music ensembles.
WWW.MANCHESTER2002-UK.COM

BRIDGEWATER HOUSE
A former warehouse on Whitworth St. Similar in size to India House and now home to a number of organizations including the British Council.
SIMON TAYLOR ET AL., *MANCHESTER: THE WAREHOUSE LEGACY* (2002).

BRIERLEY, BENJAMIN (1825–1896)
Born in Failsworth, Brierley was especially skilled at writing in Lancashire dialect and recited his work in working men's clubs. He worked as a sub-editor on the *Oldham Times* and he was an original member of the Manchester Literary Club.
WWW.MANCHESTER2002-UK.COM

BRIGHT, JOHN (1811–1889)
Mill owner from Rochdale and co-founder of the Anti Corn Law League. He was a down-to-earth and hard-working man, a Quaker orator and MP for Durham in 1843, friend and mentor of Beatrix Potter, the internationally acclaimed children's writer, and of her father, Rupert. Both Bright and Richard Cobden were unpopular for opposing the Crimean War in the mid-1850s; but he supported the North (anti-slavery) side during the American Civil War (1861–5).
Chambers Biographical Dictionary.

BRITON'S PROTECTION
Built in 1811, the pub is one of only two surviving original houses on Great Bridgewater St. It is now a traditional pub specializing in whiskies and stocks over a hundred varieties which can be used to wash down the shark, venison and rabbit dishes on offer on the menu.
WWW.MANCHESTER2002-UK.COM

BROWNSFIELD MILL
Great Ancoats St. A seven-storey mill built in an L-shape. Initially a cotton mill, it later had several different tenancies which included A V Roe, established there in 1910, who manufactured aeroplanes.
ROBINA MCNEIL AND MICHAEL NEVELL, *A GUIDE TO THE INDUSTRIAL ARCHAEOLOGY OF GREATER MANCHESTER* (2000); MIKE WILLIAMS WITH D A FARNIE, *COTTON MILLS IN GREATER MANCHESTER* (1992).

BROWN'S WAREHOUSE
Portland St. It was designed in 1854 by Edward Walters (who also designed the Free Trade Hall) with an 'arcading façade'. By 1858 the warehouse (covering 1, 3, 5, 7 and 9 Portland St) was jointly owned by Kershaw, Leese and Sidebottom, merchants, and James Brown & Co. merchants. Units were let out to a number of merchants but despite the all different names the building came to be known as Brown's. During the 20th century the warehouse was converted first to the Queen's Hotel and then the Portland Hotel. Today the building houses the Thistle Hotel and GMPTE Executive.

Queen's Hotel on corner of Portland St and Aytoun St, now Thistle Hotel and modern offices.

GLYNIS COOPER, *HIDDEN MANCHESTER* (2004); SIMON TAYLOR ET AL., *MANCHESTER: THE WAREHOUSE LEGACY* (2002).

BRUNSWICK MILL
Bradford Rd. A seven-storey cotton mill designed by David Bellhouse and built alongside the Ashton Canal in 1840. It had thirty-five loading bays facing onto the canal. By the 1850s the mill was working 276 carding machines and 77,000 mule spindles.
ROBINA MCNEIL AND MICHAEL NEVELL, *A GUIDE TO THE INDUSTRIAL ARCHAEOLOGY OF GREATER MANCHESTER* (2000); MIKE WILLIAMS WITH D A FARNIE, *COTTON MILLS IN GREATER MANCHESTER* (1992).

BURGESS, ANTHONY (1917–1993)
Writer, born in Harpurhey and educated at Xaverian College in Manchester and at Manchester University. His mother and sister died in the Spanish flu pandemic of 1919 when he was just 2. Anthony Burgess wrote over fifty novels during his career but his best known work is *A Clockwork Orange*.
WWW.MANCHESTER2002-UK.COM

BURNAGE

Known as 'the prettiest village in Manchester' in 1894. Burnage Garden Village was built 1906–12 to provide decent homes for workers, with 'light and air and pleasantness of outlook', offering 'mod cons' of hot and cold running water, electricity and bathrooms. Burnage escaped the ravages of the Industrial Revolution but became a target for German bombers in the Second World War because of the Fairey Aviation Works. Since 1945, however, there has been a good deal of housing development in the area and Burnage is now a large residential suburb. Musician brothers Noel and Liam Gallagher, founders of the rock band Oasis, hail from Burnage.

GLYNIS COOPER, *THE ILLUSTRATED HISTORY OF THE MANCHESTER SUBURBS* (2002); GAY SUSSEX ET AL., *LOOKING BACK AT LEVENSHULME AND BURNAGE* (1987).

BURNETT, FRANCES HODGSON (1849–1924)

Writer, born in Cheetham Hill Rd, the daughter of a shopkeeper, but emigrated to Tennessee with her mother to live with her brother after her father's death. Frances married a doctor but they divorced in 1898 because of conflicting work interests and her literary success. Her best known works are *Little Lord Fauntleroy* (1886) and *The Secret Garden* (1909).

WWW.MANCHESTER2002-UK.COM

BYROM, JOHN (1692–1763)

Born in the Old Wellington Inn in Manchester and educated at Merchant Taylors School and Trinity College Cambridge. He wrote articles and poems

Old Wellington Inn dating from Tudor times.

for *The Spectator* and he invented a form of shorthand which was widely used. He was a devout Jacobite and watched Bonnie Prince Charlie's entry into Manchester in 1745 from the windows of his house. Against family opposition he married his cousin who was his true love. Byrom became a Fellow of the Royal Society in 1724. He wrote poetry and religious essays but his best known work is the hymn 'Christians Awake!'.
GLYNIS COOPER, *HIDDEN MANCHESTER* (2004).

C

CAMBRIDGE STREET MILL
Chorlton-on-Medlock. One of the first iron framed mills, it was a six-storey mill with two basements and twenty loading bays, built by Hugh Birley in 1814 and enlarged in 1845. The mill was driven by a Boulton and Watt beam engine and had gas lighting. During the 1840s the mill was taken over by Charles Macintosh who, in 1823, had developed a process to waterproof cloth using by-products from gas manufacture. By the early 20th century Dunlop were working from the mill.
ROBINA MCNEIL AND MICHAEL NEVELL, *A GUIDE TO THE INDUSTRIAL ARCHAEOLOGY OF GREATER MANCHESTER* (2000); MIKE WILLIAMS WITH D A FARNIE, *COTTON MILLS IN GREATER MANCHESTER* (1992).

CANALS
The 3rd Duke of Bridgewater pioneered Manchester's canal system as a cheap and effective way of moving coals and cargoes around the North-West,

Regeneration of the canal sides at Castlefield.

alongside other canal companies. These canals carried mostly coal, corn, construction materials and, to a lesser extent, cotton.

☛ *See also* DUKE OF BRIDGEWATER'S CANAL; ASHTON CANAL; ROCHDALE CANAL; BOLTON AND BURY CANAL; MANCHESTER AND SALFORD JUNCTION CANAL; LOST CANAL.

WWW.SPINNINGTHEWEB.ORG.UK

CARDUS, NEVILLE (B. 1895)

He was born in Sumner Place Rusholme and used the Free Library to educate himself. He wrote about his two enthusiasms, cricket and music, and he became a critic on cricket and music for the *Manchester Guardian*. Neville Cardus was knighted in 1967.

WWW.MANCHESTER2002-UK.COM

CARTIMANDUA

Queen Cartimandua of the Brigantes was one of only two Celtic Queens in their own right (the other being Boudicca of the Iceni). As the Brigantian Queen, Cartimandua, like Boudicca, might have been expected to be implacably opposed to the Romans but in fact she actively co-operated with them; though this may have been born out of a desire to rid herself of her hated husband, Caractacus, rather than for motives of appeasement or trade. In return for her co-operation the Romans obliged by keeping Caractacus in chains and under house arrest in Rome until his death. Cartimandua was then free to marry Venutius, the Roman overlord of York, with whom she had fallen in love. However after a while he betrayed her in turn by switching allegiance to the Brigantes.

The legend of Queen Cartimandua has survived for nearly 2,000 years and during the late 19th or early 20th century a stone head in a supposed likeness of Cartimandua was found near Manchester. If the likeness was truthful then she was a pretty queen. There is a Celtic stone head tradition in the Manchester area and it is believed that if a likeness of a person was carved then that person could continue to communicate with the living after their death. Cartimandua is still remembered for her betrayal of her people and her husband, though it is not clear what the creators of her stone likeness centuries later had hoped to achieve. The head disappeared over thirty years ago and it is unlikely that the reasons for her commemoration in this way will ever be known.

MANCHESTER MUSEUM, OXFORD RD.

CASTLEFIELD

The original fort at Castlefield was built by Agricola in AD 79 on a spur of land where the Rivers Irwell and Medlock met. It was called Mamceaster

Restored defensive wall at Castlefield Roman fort in Manchester.

Jackson's Wharf in former canal warehouse, now a fish restaurant , at Castlefield.

(mam from the Celtic name for hill and ceaster derived from the Latin word for a walled town) The fort was about five acres in size and guarded important routeways to and from Chester, York and the Cheshire salt wiches. There were three main phases of fort building. The first fort (from AD 79 to c.110–25) was built of timber and turf, with two defensive ditches on three sides and the river to the south providing a defensive measure on the fourth side. Opposite the river the north gate was guarded by two wooden towers. A second larger fort was built c.160 and the north gate was blocked by a ditch. The final phase saw a stone fort of a similar plan replace the turf and timber structure c.200 and this remained in use until the Romans abandoned Britain in 410. During the last two hundred years of the fort's occupation seventeen changes were made to the defensive ditches, suggesting turbulent times. Pottery-making and metal-working evidence have been found in the area of the vicus, a civilian settlement adjacent to the site.

The roads, railways and canals of the Industrial Revolution destroyed most of the surface remains of the fort and the vicus. All that survive are a few hummocks and a section of wall. A small area of the former fort, together with part of the curtain wall, a modern interpretation of a Roman watch tower and the north gate, has been reconstructed to give some idea of what the original would have been like and the gate bears an inscription

BARCA, Castlefield, under the arches, where local celebrities go for a drink.

commemorating the troops from Spain, Austria and Romania who served at Mamceastre under their centurion, Lucius Senecianus Martius, *c.200.* WWW.GMAU.ORG/; WWW.ART.MAN.AC.UK/FIELDARCHAEOLOGYCENTRE/; THE CASTLEFIELD MANAGEMENT CO., CASTLEFIELD CENTRE, 101 LIVERPOOL ROAD, CASTLEFIELD, MANCHESTER M3 4JN.

CATHEDRAL CHURCH OF ST MARY, ST DENYS AND ST GEORGE

The first church in Manchester was built around the 7th century. Evidence for this early church comes from the 'Angel Stone' discovered embedded in the wall of the south porch during the 19th century. The stone bears a rough carving of what appears to be an angel together with an inscription which reads 'into thy hands, O Lord, I commend my spirit'. The Saxon church may have stood at what is now the corner of St Mary's Gate and Exchange St, which agrees with evidence that there are the remains of a 10th-century graveyard in the vicinity of St Ann's Square. However, this church was destroyed by the Danes during the Viking invasions.

Manchester Cathedral Church of St Mary, St Denys and St George, c.1910.

Manchester Cathedral Church of St Mary, St Denys and St George c. 2003.

The present cathedral church has evolved from the church built by Edward the Elder in 923 after recapturing Manchester from the Vikings; and this is the St Mary's church mentioned by Domesday Book in 1086.

In 1215 the present church was built in perpendicular Gothic style within the Baron de Grelley's Court (beside the manor house which today is Chetham's College) and dedicated by Henry V to St Mary, St Denys and St George. Around 1311 the de Grelley family built and endowed St Nicholas's Chantry.

The barony passed to the de la Warre family in 1398 and in 1421 Thomas de la Warre, Lord of Manchester, obtained the status of collegiate college for the church. He rebuilt the manor house along the lines of a small college which would house a warden, eight fellows, four clerks, and six lay choristers.

Additions and alterations continued to be made to the church over the next two hundred years; perhaps most notably the Minstrel Angels commissioned by Lady Margaret Beaufort, mother of Henry Tudor (Henry VII) who in 1482 had married Sir Thomas Stanley, brother of James Stanley, warden of the collegiate college. There are also a number of fine medieval woodcarvings crafted by the Ripon Woodcarvers between 1485 and 1506.

The college was closed down in 1547 after the Dissolution of the Monasteries; refounded during the reign of the Catholic Queen Mary Tudor (1553–8); closed down again when she died and eventually re-established as Christ's College in 1578 under Queen Elizabeth I. The church and college were ransacked during the Civil War (1640–9) and the college was left semi-derelict. It was bought by Humphrey Chetham in 1653 who established Chetham's College which survives to this day.

The collegiate church attained cathedral status in 1847. Inside the church had changed little but much of the exterior was a 19th-century reconstruction by Joseph Crowther. In 1940, during the Blitz by the German Luftwaffe, the Cathedral sustained a direct hit and suffered severe damage. Many of the beautiful glass windows were blown to bits but the choir stalls and misericords (choir seats) and most of the fine carved woodwork survived, along with some 8th-century stone fragments and the piers supporting the tower which dated from 1380. A Fire Window by Margaret Traherne is installed near to the site of the impact and there are five windows by Tony Holloway on the west side of the Cathedral depicting St Mary, St Denys, St George, Genesis and Revelations.

WWW.MANCHESTERCATHEDRAL.ORG/

CELTIC MANCHESTER

Celtic tribes arrived in Britain *c.*500 BC and never left. The River Medlock (meadow stream) is a Celtic name and the Celtic tribe of the Brigantes made their home on the sandstone outcrop where the Irk and the Medlock meet and on which the Cathedral stands today. The site offered a good defensive position, supplies of water were easily accessible and the surrounding woods proved fertile hunting grounds. The Brigantes practised guerrilla warfare tactics which proved extremely successful against the Romans; but the Brigantes were not averse to trading with the latter when they were not fighting against them.

GLYNIS COOPER, *ILLUSTRATED HISTORY OF THE MANCHESTER SUBURBS* (2002).

CENTRAL LIBRARY

An innovative four-storey circular building designed by E. Vincent Harris (who also designed the adjacent Town Hall extension in 1937) which was completed and opened in 1934 by King George V and Queen Mary. The library stands over the culverted River Tib on the site from which the 28th and 31st Infantry advanced on the hapless folk caught in the Peterloo Massacre of 1819. The fine porticoed main entrance faces St Peter's Square.

Central Library, St Peters Square.

On the ground floor are the European and business libraries as well as a general lending library for fiction, biography and children's books. The first floor houses social sciences and humanities, local studies, the scientific library and 'Networks' (public computers for accessing the 'information super highway').

Henry Watson's renowned music library is on the second floor; the unique Chinese library and the arts library are on the third floor; while the top floor is occupied by languages and literature plus a formidable collection of local studies images, over half of which have been digitized for public access.

The library recently celebrated 150 years of public library service (albeit not in the same building) and has done more than live up to Charles Dickens's description of its 1850s predecessor as 'a great free school'.
WWW.MANCHESTER.GOV.UK/LIBRARIES

CENTRAL STATION (GMEX)
Lower Mosley St. Manchester to Liverpool services, Cheshire Lines, Great Northern and the old Midland Railways operated out of this station. The Midland Hotel was built to cater for railway passengers. The station was closed in the late 1960s following Dr Beeching's 'rationalization' of the railways. By the mid-1980s it had been refurbished at a cost of £20million to become one of the country's largest exhibition centres, covering 10,000 square metres. The 'vast vaulted roof' is said to be held up by 'sheer engineering ingenuity and simple geometry'. Exhibitions, fairs and performances are held regularly; and Torvill and Dean staged an ice spectacular there.
ALAN KIDD, *HISTORY OF MANCHESTER* (3RD EDN, 2002); WWW.MANCHESTER 2002-UK.COM

CHARLTON, BOBBY (B. 1937)
A miner's son from County Durham, Bobby Charlton joined Manchester United after winning England schoolboy international honours. He played as a forward for United from 1956 to 1973, surviving the Munich air crash of 1958; and won a record 106 England caps. In 1966 he was a member of the England World Cup winning team and he was also voted Footballer of the Year. After his retirement from the active game he became manager of Preston North End and was knighted for services to football in 1994.
WWW.MANCHESTER2002-UK.COM

CHEETHAM
Today Cheetham is unrecognizable as 'the village by the wood' where the 'air was sweet with the perfume of roses, pinks, carnations, migonette' because 'the open countryside of the 1820s was a solid mass of bricks and mortar by the 1870s'. It was at Stocks House, on the corner of Cheetham Hill Rd and North

Rd, that Charles Dickens met the Grant brothers on whom he modelled the Cheeryble Bothers in his novel *Nicholas Nickelby*. Strangeways Hall, which stood in its own beautiful parkland, was demolished by 1863 and the New Assize Courts (designed by Alfred Waterhouse) opened in 1864. Strangeways Prison was built behind the courts in the former grounds of the Hall and became operational in 1868. The area around the prison is rather drab and full of sell-direct-to-the-public textile warehouses. At 20 Cheetham Hill Rd Michael Marks opened a penny bazaar in 1893. The following year he went into partnership with Tom Spencer and Marks and Spencer was born.

Cheetham had a large Jewish community and several synagogues were built to cater for their religious needs. Since the 1980s there has been a population shift and the area now has a predominantly Asian community. Many of the synagogues closed down but the Spanish and Portuguese Synagogue, built in 1874, closed for worship in 1982 and reopened in 1984 as a Jewish Museum. Cheetham was also renowned for Boddingtons Brewery (Boddies Gold is a favourite beer in the North-West) but, after over a hundred years of brewing in Cheetham, the brewery closed in 2004. On a lighter note, in Victorian times Cheetham was home to a medical practitioner by the name of Dr Body.

☛ *See also* ALFRED WATERHOUSE; JEWISH MUSEUM; MARKS AND SPENCER.
GLYNIS COOPER, *THE ILLUSTRATED HISTORY OF THE MANCHESTER SUBURBS* (2002).

CHEETHAM AND BROUGHTON PARTNERSHIP

Regeneration scheme to revitalize Cheetham and Broughton which have suffered from population shifts, loss of business and urban graffiti.
ALAN KIDD, *HISTORY OF MANCHESTER* (3RD EDN, 2002); WWW.MANCHESTER 2002-UK.COM

CHEETHAM GHOST

A certain house in Cheetham, the exact location of which is no longer known, was haunted by 'a child's cries and a mournful whistling … and the apparitions of an old woman and a black figure'. Mediums were called and in response to messages which they received 'a search of the house revealed a narrow strip of calico sheeting in a chimney, copies of 1922 newspapers and a pencilled musical score similar to the tune whistled'. Subsequently some small bones were discovered beneath the kitchen floor. The police insisted that they belonged to a cat or rabbit, and that they were not those of a small baby as at first believed; though they could not explain how they had come to be under the floor or why they should have been buried there. This particular mystery was never solved.
PETER UNDERWOOD, *THE A–Z OF BRITISH GHOSTS* (1971).

CHETHAM, HUMPHREY (1580–1653)

Born at Crumpsall Hall in 1580 and educated at Manchester Grammar School, Chetham was a wealthy merchant and became High Sheriff of Lancashire in 1635. In 1620 he bought the moated manor house of Clayton Hall and made it his home. It was his ambition to benefit scholars and help poor children and in 1651 he began negotiations for the former collegiate college buildings which were semi-derelict. Although he died before these were completed, the strict instructions he left in his will were carried out. His fortune was to 'be used to endow a hospital for the maintenance and education of forty poor boys' and to 'adapt and equip part of the library for the use of scholars'.

☞ *See also* CHETHAM'S LIBRARY.
WWW.MANCHESTER2002-UK.COM

CHETHAM'S LIBRARY

Cathedral Gardens. Chetham's was one of the first public libraries in the world. The library was established with a bequest of a thousand pounds from Humphrey Chetham who died in 1653. It is housed in the former collegiate college buildings which stood on the site of the 13th-century manor house.

The reading room is in what would probably have been a master bedroom. It is a quiet spacious wood-panelled room with a portrait of Humphrey Chetham hanging over the large fireplace. In an attempt to retain a cosy feel there are no rows of reading desks, just a well polished oval table in the centre of the room around which are ranged a dozen chairs. It was here that

Medieval gatehouse at Chetham's College.

Karl Marx and Friedrich Engels worked on their *Communist Manifesto* in the mid-19th century; and the place has remained little changed except for a small PC tucked away in the corner from which the library catalogues can be accessed. The collections are catalogued chronologically. In another corner the Gorton chained library is kept in a locked wooden bookcase; but most of the library's books are held in large wooden presses ranged along the Priests Wing and the Mary Chapel Wing. There are also a number of specialist collections which include the archives of the Peterloo Massacre and Belle Vue Gardens.

Chetham's Library is still open to the public from Monday to Friday by prior arrangement of twenty-four hours notice to the librarian. Enquiries can be made at the entrance by the old medieval gatehouse. There are guided tours of the buildings available for groups and individuals. Also part of the former collegiate college buildings is Chetham's School of Music and weekly concerts, open to the public, are held in the old baronial hall.

☛ *See also* HUMPHREY CHETHAM; JOHN DEE; PETERLOO; CATHEDRAL CHURCH OF ST MARY, ST DENYS AND ST GEORGE.
WWW.CHETHAMS.ORG.UK; GLYNIS COOPER, *HIDDEN MANCHESTER* (2003).

CHINA TOWN

Increasingly Chinese immigrants have been coming to England over the last sixty years or so. Initially Chinese laundries were popular but with the growth of domestic washing machines the Chinese have diversified into Chinese restaurants, medicine and art. Faulkner St, once at the heart of the English business community, is now the centre of what has become known as China Town. The street is dominated by a beautiful red and gold Chinese arch decorated with dragons and phoenixes, said to be symbols of luck and prosperity. The arch was built in 1987 and 'is the first true Imperial Chinese arch erected in Europe'. At the same time

Chinese Arch, surrounded by former Victorian warehouses, in Faulkner St, the hub of China Town.

a pagoda was built in the street, a Chinese garden planted and a life-size mural of a junk painted on a brick wall. It was a celebration of Chinese life and culture, the making of a little piece of China in England. Chinese financial and legal services and health centres lie alongside food shops and restaurants centred on China Town. The Chinese Arts Centre used to be here too, but it has now moved to Thomas St, 10–15 minutes walk away.
GLYNIS COOPER, *HIDDEN MANCHESTER* (2004); WWW.MANCHESTER2002-UK.COM

CHORLTON-CUM-HARDY
Chorlton lies on the western edge of Manchester's suburbs and grew up as a settlement close to the water meadows of the Mersey. In the 19th century Chorlton remained rural while the inner suburbs fell victim to the millscapes. Victorian farms in Chorlton had some delightfully evocative field names such as Tongue Shaped Piece; Great Raids Bungs; Burnt Earth and Back o' t' World. The oldest part of Chorlton is centred around the Green and there are still rural echoes here. Before the footbridge was built there was 'a ferry cross the Mersey' from Jackson's Boat, better known as the Bridge Inn. Barlow Moor Aerodrome, Manchester's first airport, was built during the early 1930s on Hough End Fields, part of Hough End Hall estate, a former peacock farm, which stood on Eddisbury Ave.
GLYNIS COOPER, *THE ILLUSTRATED HISTORY OF THE MANCHESTER SUBURBS* (2002); JOHN LLOYD, *LOOKING BACK AT CHORLTON-CUM-HARDY* (1985).

CHORLTON EES
Chorlton-cum-Hardy. The Ees is a water park established under the Red Rose Forest Scheme and lies on land formerly occupied by Barlow Hall Farm, which stood on the boundaries of Chorlton. The River Mersey (from the Anglo-Saxon 'Maeres-Eea' from which the name Ees is derived) runs through the fields and copses of the water park and there is a large lake in a gravel pit excavated for building the M63 motorway during the 1970s. The woodlands and water meadows provide an excellent habitat for flora and fauna, while the lake is full of pike, carp, tench, roach, perch and bream.
WWW.MANCHESTER2003-UK.COM

CHORLTON-ON-MEDLOCK
A very central suburb and often indistinguishable from Manchester city centre. Its origins go back to Viking times when it was a small village lying on the banks of the Medlock. Chorlton Hall was built in the first part of the 17th century and by 1800 the population was still only 675. With the impact of the Industrial Revolution this multiplied over thirty times in thirty years to 20,569. During the next thirty years the population doubled again and by

1891 had reached over 60,000. The Chorlton St mills complex, bounded by Oxford St, Cambridge St, Chester St and the River Medlock, included the Oxford Rd Twist Mill (built 1803 by Samuel Marsland and demolished 1930), and Macintosh's Works on Cambridge St. In 1823 Charles Macintosh developed a process to waterproof cloth using by-products from gas manufacture. This factory eventually became Dunlop.

Little Ireland was tucked into a 'bow' in the River Medlock and gained a notorious reputation for the cramped, dark, damp and squalid conditions in which thousands of Irish migrant workers lived. Today the ecofriendly Macintosh Village developed by Taylor Woodrow stands on the site.

The streets on the edge of the suburb were somewhat more refined. The novelist, Elizabeth Gaskell, lived with her Unitarian minister husband, William, at 84 Plymouth Grove, while the home of suffragette Emmeline Pankhurst and her family was at 62 Nelson St nearby. David Lloyd George was born at 5 New York Terrace in January 1863 and was made a Freeman of the City of Manchester in 1918. Chorlton-on-Medlock Town Hall (built 1830, demolished 1970s) had its moment of fame in 1945 when a Pan African Congress was held. Delegates included Jomo Kenyatta and Kwame Nkrumah.

Today the whole area has been redeveloped and is characterized by the Universities (Manchester Victoria and Manchester Metropolitan) on Oxford Rd; the BBC and Manchester Museum, also on Oxford Rd; the Manchester Eye Hospital and St Mary's Maternity Hospital.

GLYNIS COOPERR, *THE ILLUSTRATED HISTORY OF THE MANCHESTER SUBURBS* (2002); CHRIS MAKEPEACE, *LOOKING BACK AT HULME, MOSS SIDE, CHORLTON-ON -MEDLOCK AND ARDWICK* (1998).

CHRISTIES HOSPITAL

Christies opened in 1932 and is a hospital which specializes in the treatment of cancer and stands side by side with the Holt Radium Institute on Wilmslow Rd in Withington.

GLYNIS COOPER, *THE ILLUSTRATED HISTORY OF THE MANCHESTER SUBURBS* (2002); WWW.CMHT.NWEST.NHS.UK/HOSPITALS

CHURCHES

It is impossible to cover all churches in Manchester past and present in this book; they would require a volume to themselves. Full details of places of worship can be accessed via the website www.manchester2002-uk.com.

☛ *See also* CATHEDRAL CHURCH; ST ANN'S CHURCH; HIDDEN GEM; ST FRANCIS MONASTIC CHURCH; ST GEORGE'S CHURCH; ST JAMES CHURCH; CHURCH OF THE HOLY NAME; FIRST CHURCH OF CHRIST SCIENTIST; ALL SAINTS; FRIENDS MEETING HOUSE; ST NICHOLAS CHURCH; CROSS STREET UNITARIAN CHURCH.

CHURCH OF THE HOLY NAME
Oxford Rd, Chorlton-on-Medlock. This fine Roman Catholic church was designed and built by Joseph Hanson and his son in 1869–71. The octagonal tower top was added later by Adrian Scott in 1928. The outer façade is asymmetrical and the interior is light and spacious with 'slender columns and light rib vaulted ceiling of terra cotta'. There are chapels on either side of the chancel and stained glass windows. A number of life-sized plaster statues around the church were created by the sculptor Alberti in 1900. Today the church lies at the heart of the University campus. There were fears that it would be demolished in the 1960s to make way for the medical school but after interventions by architectural expert Professor Nikolaus Pevsner and a number of local people the building was given Grade II listed status and the medical school was built a little further down Oxford Rd. One of the most high-profile funerals held in the church was that of the actress Pat Phoenix who was celebrated for playing Elsie Tanner in *Coronation St.*
WWW.MANCHESTER2002-UK.COM

CIRCUS TAVERN
Portland St. Built about 1790, it is said to be the smallest pub in Manchester and has one of the smallest bars in Britain. In the 18th century Portland St attracted street entertainers and artistes due to perform at the circus in nearby Chatham St.
WWW.MANCHESTER2002-UK.COM

CLARKE, WARREN (B. 1948)
Warren Clarke was born in Chorlton-cum-Hardy and worked for the *Manchester Evening News* after leaving school. He took up amateur dramatics and then became a professional actor. Stage performances include Manchester Library Theatre. He has appeared in a number of film and television roles including Dim in *A Clockwork Orange* and Dalziel in *Dalziel and Pascoe*.
WWW.MANCHESTER2002-UK.COM

CLAYTON
Clayton is noted for having Manchester's only surviving example of a moated manor house. Dating from the 12th century, it was rebuilt in Tudor times by ancestors of the 19th-century poet, Lord Byron, as a black and white timbered hall. The family was friendly with Dr John Dee, the Elizabethan mathematician and astrologer. Humphrey Chetham, founder of Chetham's College and Library, bought the Hall in 1620 and lived there until his death in 1663. Today the Hall is a private dwelling, surrounded by a modern housing estate and almost obliterated from public view by St Cross Church on Ashton New Rd.

Clayton stands close to the Ashton Canal and during the 19th century was home to chemical and engineering works. It is currently part of the East Manchester Regeneration Scheme and the stadium built for the Commonwealth Games in 2002 dominates the local landscape; but Clayton also has the unenviable reputation of being a base for the armed response teams of Greater Manchester Police.

☞ *See also* CLAYTON HALL.

GLYNIS COOPER, *THE ILLUSTRATED HISTORY OF THE MANCHESTER SUBURBS* (2002); KAREN HOPES, *CLAYTON MEMORIES* (2001).

COBDEN, RICHARD (1804–1865)

Manchester mill owner who helped to found the Anti Corn Law League (which protested against the high price of corn and therefore bread, and called for a reform in the law). Cobden built the first Italian palazzo style of warehouse on Mosley St in 1839 for his textiles. However, he was so politically active that he neglected his business and suffered severe financial hardship. Widely travelled, he became MP for Stockport and the West Riding. In 1851 Owens College, which was to form the basis of Manchester University in 1902, was set up in his former house on Quay St.

CHAMBERS BIOGRAPHICAL DICTIONARY.

COBDEN'S WAREHOUSE

Mosley St. During the 1840s the Italian 'palazzo' style of warehouse, inspired by the Renaissance architecture of Florence and Venice, became popular. The first one built in Manchester in this style was designed by Edward Walters and was built by Richard Cobden on Mosley St in 1839. His friend and colleague Edmund Potter took over the warehouse for his rapidly expanding business in printed calicoes. The warehouse has survived changing fortunes and two world wars and is today home to Lloyds TSB Bank at 14–16 Mosley St. Edward Walters also built another warehouse in this style at 36 Charlotte St.

GLYNIS COOPER, *HIDDEN MANCHESTER* (2004); SIMON TAYLOR ET AL., *MANCHESTER: THE WAREHOUSE LEGACY* (2002).

CODE, JOHN HENRY DCM (1869–1934)

Local man who worked as a carpenter at Clayton Gas Works. He enlisted in the 5th Ardwick Volunteer Battalion of the Manchester Regiment in 1886 and was promoted to sergeant in 1890. He won the Singleton Trophy for sharp shooting. John Code took part in the Boer War and then the First World War. He was posted to Gallipoli in 1914 and it was while on active service there that he won the DCM. He was then appointed regimental quartermaster sergeant. After the war he returned to Clayton Gas Works until

he retired. In 1920 he founded St Andrew's Ladies Hockey Team where both his daughters played for several years.
WWW.MANCHESTER2002-UK.COM

COLLEGE OF ART
All Saints, Oxford Rd. It was established as the Manchester College of Art and Design in 1838 and moved to a new building at All Saints on Oxford Rd in 1881. The College was extended in 1898 and today forms part of the Victoria University of Manchester.
GLYNIS COOPER, *THE ILLUSTRATED HISTORY OF THE MANCHESTER SUBURBS* (2002).

COLLYHURST
The original settlement site at Collyhurst was on a red sandstone hill known locally as Red Bank. Stone was quarried from the site for the construction of the later phases of the Roman fort at Castlefield and for the rebuilding of Manchester Parish Church (now the Cathedral) during the 15th century. Opencast mining was also carried out locally as early as 1322.

Collyhurst had large areas of common pasture land, some of which survived until the 1840s. Six acres of this land near Collyhurst Clough were used for burials of victims of the Black Death. Human remains in a lead coffin were found in the clough during construction work on Rochdale Rd in 1806. Plague can remain active for hundreds of years and it was good fortune that the grazing use of the land did not succeed in reactivating the Plague.

Collyhurst Common was a popular spot for archery practice. Around 1650, amid concern that archery skills were in decline, a law was passed which required every male over the age of 7 to own a bow and at least two shafts of arrows. Practice had to be carried out at least four times a year by every man and boy. The local Court Leet (a kind of magistrate's court) dealt severely with those who did not comply.

During the Industrial Revolution the former cottage industries of bleaching and dyeing mushroomed. Chemical works and half a dozen dye works stood on the local river banks. St Georges Collieries in the Osborne St area made the whole place grimy with coal dust. This was worsened by the coming of the railways. 'Railways made heavy demands in Collyhurst, soaring brick viaducts were slung along the Irk valley, adding gloominess and more pollution to the trapped atmosphere below' (A J Dobbs, 1978).

Today Collyhurst maybe a tad cleaner but the population has declined, although there are modern Corporation housing estates, a business park on Oldham Rd and a water works by the railway.

☛ *See also GIANT CUCUMBER; GHOST OF TOPLEY STREET.*
GLYNIS COOPER, *THE ILLUSTRATED HISTORY OF THE MANCHESTER SUBURBS* (2002); ALLAN D BARLOW, *A HISTORY OF COLLYHURST AND HARPURHEY* (1977).

COMMONWEALTH GAMES

Manchester staged a successful Commonwealth Games in 2002 in the new purpose-built City of Manchester Stadium at Sportcity, part of the East Manchester Regeneration Scheme. The Queen attended both the Opening and Closing Ceremonies. The Games 'ran for ten days from Friday 26th July to Sunday 4th August. Seventeen sports were represented with over 4000 competitors coming from 72 nations within the British Commonwealth ... around one million visitors are thought to have come to Manchester to see the event live and the world television audience was estimated to top one billion'.

WWW.MANCHESTER2002-UK.COM

Manchester's celebration of the Commonwealth Games 2002, Piccadilly.

COMPUTERS

In 1935 Professor Douglas Hartree developed a differential analyser to solve mathematical equations quickly. Metropolitan Vickers in Trafford manufactured the model to his specifications. Building on his work, staff at the University of Manchester developed 'The Baby' in 1948. It was the first modern computer.

Europe's first commercial computer was built by Ferranti at West Gorton in 1950 and delivered to the University. The Mark 1 Star was based on the developmental work done at Manchester University during the 1940s. The machine filled two bays 4.8m long by 2.4m deep by 1.2 m high. It had 4,000 valves and needed 27kw of electricity to work. This was followed by the Ferranti Pegasus 1 built in 1957 for Vickers Aircraft.

W H MAYALL, CHALLENGE OF THE CHIP (1979); MUSEUM OF SCIENCE AND INDUSTRY, WWW.MSIM.ORG.UK

CONTACT THEATRE

Oxford Rd/Devas St. This octagonal theatre is part of Manchester University. One of the most memorable performances was of Raymond Briggs's play *When the Wind Blows* when an attempt was made to simulate the aftermath of a nuclear bomb explosion. The theatre was plunged into complete darkness and wind machines were turned on the audience before images of a fire storm were flashed onto the walls. The theatre was totally renovated in 1999 and is one of the most innovative Manchester theatres, staging mostly modern works for young audiences.

HTTP://WWW.CONTACT-THEATRE.ORG;

COOKE, ALISTAIR, KBE (1908–2004)

Born in Manchester and educated at Cambridge University, Alistair Cooke went on to become a well-known journalist, writer, commentator and broadcaster. His programme, *Letter from America*, which he began broadcasting in 1946 on the BBC Home Service (now Radio 4) became a national institution and he presented it for 58 years until his death in 2004.

WWW.MANCHESTER2002-UK.COM

COTTON BOARD

The Cotton Board, now disbanded, was set up to promote and market British cotton in fashion after the post-war slumps. It became a noted 'pressure group' along with its sister organization the Colour Style and Design Centre. Fashion shows were held during the 1950s and 1960s to emphasize the versatility of cotton and its benefits. Many of the outfits from these shows were later presented to the Gallery of Costume at Platt Hall. The photographic collection is held by the Greater Manchester Record Office.

WWW.MANCHESTERGALLERIES.ORG; WWW.GMCRO.CO.UK

COTTON QUEENS

In 1930 a national Cotton Queen competition was started to encourage interest in the cotton industry. It was an annual three-week event held in Blackpool and the winner would spend a year travelling around the country promoting cotton at exhibitions, fashion parades, public events and organizations.

The first winner was a 19-year-old girl from Glossop named Frances Lockett. She worked at a mill in Hyde and recalled the excitement and the events she attended.

I did mannequin parades, they had cotton balls, cotton weeks at Lewis's and Kendals, and I went all over Great Britain … I went to the Houses of Parliament and I had lunch with six cabinet ministers. Mr Ramsay McDonald was the Prime Minister and I had an interview with him He said he wished he was coming to the Cotton Ball that night. We had a ball at Covent Garden. Then I met Mr [David] Lloyd George. He had a feel at my dress and he said 'Is this cotton?' I said 'Oh yes'. He said 'It's lovely … I must get Megan to buy some of this.'

TAMESIDE LOCAL STUDIES DEPT ASHTON-UNDER-LYNE; WWW.SPINNINGTHEWEB. ORG.UK.

COW TRAIL

In the summer of 2004 Manchester City Council took part in the world's largest public art exhibition, the Cowparade. Along with cities like New York,

Fountain on St Ann's Square and Lake Land Belle from the Cow Trail.

Zurich and Sydney, 150 individually painted life-size fibreglass models of cows were placed across the city on a Cow Trail. The Council particularly wanted to involve residents in regeneration areas with working with local artists in 'cow-munity' schemes to produce some members of the herd. There were also moo-walks around the cow trail to see the results of 'over a year of planning, dedication, tears and laughter'. The model cows were very life-like and an excellent talking point; and some of them were real characters. MANCHESTER CITY COUNCIL COW TRAIL MAP.

CROMWELL, OLIVER
During the Civil War (1640–9) Manchester was a Roundhead Parliamentary stronghold. In 1875 Matthew Noble's statue of Oliver Cromwell, said to be a realistic likeness of him, was erected close to Manchester Cathedral. It faced Exchange Station and showed him in full battledress with drawn sword. This upset many people, including the Irish population, who had strong folk

Exchange Station with statue of Oliver Cromwell which now stands in the grounds of Wythenshawe Hall.

memories of Cromwell's harshness and cruelty in Ireland, and Queen Victoria. When she was invited to open the new Town Hall she said she would only consent if the offending statue was removed. The statue was not moved, the Queen refused to open the Town Hall and the ceremony was performed by the Lord Mayor. The statue was finally moved as part of redevelopment schemes during the 1980s and now stands outside Wythenshawe Hall in Wythenshawe Park.
WWW.MANCHESTER2002-UK.COM

CROSS STREET
Runs from Corporation St and Market St to Albert Square. Features Cross St Unitarian Chapel, the Royal Exchange and Mr Thomas's Chop House.
☛ *See also* CROSS STREET UNITARIAN CHAPEL; MR THOMAS'S CHOP HOUSE.
MANCHESTER A–Z (2002)

CROSS STREET UNITARIAN CHAPEL
The Act of Uniformity in 1662 required that all clergymen followed the Book of Common Prayer. Some refused and were sacked by their churches. The Revd Henry Newcome was one and he and his supporters built their own 'Dissenters' meeting house, later known as Cross St Chapel, which opened in 1694. The Chapel was destroyed by German bombers in 1940 and rebuilt in 1959. The present very modern glass and chrome chapel, designed for the 21st century, was built in 1997.

From 1828 to 1884 Revd William Gaskell was the minister for Cross St Chapel. His wife was the novelist Elizabeth Gaskell who wrote *Mary Barton* and *North and South* based on the appalling conditions suffered by workers in the 19th-century millscapes. The Gaskell Society meet at Cross St Chapel regularly and there is a Gaskell Room at the Chapel which holds a collection of Gaskell memorabilia and early editions of her novels. Outside the North-West she is perhaps better known for works such as *Cranford* and *Wives and Daughters*.

The Gaskells were friendly with the Potters who were calico printers. Edmund Potter worshipped at Cross St Chapel from his boyhood and William Gaskell tutored his son, Rupert. The Gaskells often visited the Potters at their Derbyshire home and it is said that the character of John Thornley in *North and South* was based on Edmund Potter. William Gaskell was very fond of Beatrix, Edmund's granddaughter, and she of him, and he was often more of a father to her than her own father.
WWW.TBNS.NET/CROSS-STREET/

CROWN COURT
Minshull St. Originally known as the City Police and Sessions Courts, the Court was designed and built of red brick in the Florentine style by Thomas

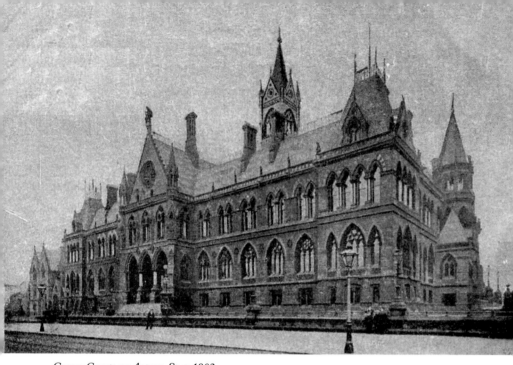

Crown Courts on Aytoun St, c.1902.

Crown Courts from Minshull St.

Worthington in 1871. It has an imposing bell tower and stands adjacent to Catalan Square. The Rochdale Canal runs along the southern flank of the building. A sign of the times is the special wheelchair lift installed by the imposing front steps.

WWW.MANCHESTER2002-UK.COM

CRUMPSALL

Humphrey Chetham, who founded Chetham's Hospital and endowed Chetham's Library, was born at Crumpsall Hall (which lay just off Crescent Rd) in 1580. A ruined thatched cottage of some considerable age was still standing in 1920 on the site of what is now Springfield Hospital. This cottage was said to have been the birthplace of Hugh Oldham who founded Manchester Grammar School in 1515.

Crumpsall escaped the real ravages of the millscapes. ICI established a large factory there and the suburb was also the headquarters of CWS Biscuit manufacture. There is a now good local arts scene based on the Abraham Moss Theatre and the Abraham Moss Centre.

 See also HUMPHREY CHETHAM

GLYNIS COOPER, *THE ILLUSTRATED HISTORY OF THE MANCHESTER SUBURBS* (2002); CRUMPSALL LIBRARY, *A REMEMBRANCE OF THINGS PAST* ... (1972).

CWS BISCUIT WORKS

The biscuit-making factory for the Co-operative Wholesale Society stood near St Thomas's School on Harpurhey Rd in Crumpsall. The works used to distribute tins of boiled sweets and biscuits to the school as a gesture of goodwill and also to thank the boisterous schoolchildren for not vandalizing the premises. Coal carts serving the biscuit works used Springfield as a route to the works because Delaunays Rd was so steep that chain horses had to pull the carts up.

GLYNIS COOPER, *ILLUSTRATED HISTORY OF THE MANCHESTER SUBURBS* (2002).

D

DALE WAREHOUSE

One of the oldest warehouses in Manchester stands in the Piccadilly Basin on the Rochdale Canal close to the junction with the Ashton Canal. A four-storey stone warehouse built in 1806, it actually looks much older. The arches where the narrow-boats and horse-drawn wagons entered are still clearly visible, and so are the goods doors and hoists.

GLYNIS COOPER, *HIDDEN MANCHESTER* (2004); SIMON TAYLOR ET AL., *MANCHESTER: THE WAREHOUSE LEGACY* (2002).

DALTON, JOHN (1776–1844)

A Manchester teacher who, in 1794, was the first person to describe colour blindness (Daltonism). He was also a renowned chemist who did much pioneering work on atomic theory. In 1799 he became a professor in mathematics and natural philosophy at the New College in Mosley St and published his first book *Meteorological Observations and Essays*, defining his fundamental laws of chemistry. Dalton joined the Literary and Philosophical Society, where he delivered his first paper on colour blindness followed by essays on his discoveries about the constitution of gases, evaporation, heat expansion, meteorology and steam power. Further work led to the formation of atomic theory, for which he is best known.

CHAMBERS BIOGRAPHICAL DICTIONARY.

DANCER, JOHN (1812–1887)

London-born Dancer moved to Manchester in 1841 to set up as an optician and instrument maker at a premises at 43 Cross St. He invented micro-photography, and he was also an eminent optician and microscope maker and made many precision instruments for James Prescott Joule.

☛ *See also JAMES PRESCOTT JOULE*

WWW.MANCHESTER2002-UK.COM

DANELAW MANCHESTER

In AD 870 the Viking invaders sailed up the Mersey and savagely destroyed Mamceastre, despite the inhabitants' vain attempts at defence by the building of the Nico Ditch, a defensive earthwork which stretched from Ashton to Chorlton-cum-Hardy. It ran through Reddish, by Levenshulme Print Works, across Stockport Rd, along Slade Lane to Birch Farm, through Longsight and Platt Fields in Rusholme to Hough Moss. In 871 there was a battle against the Danish princes Guthrum, Oscitel and Amund, who had defeated King Alfred in Wessex; and sometime later a decisive battle took place at Ryder Brow (alternatively known as Winning Hill) in Gorton. Part of the Nico Ditch is still visible in Gorton. The Danes remained in the area for about forty years and imposed a tax known as the Danegeld on the Saxons.

GLYNIS COOPER, *ILLUSTRATED HISTORY OF THE MANCHESTER SUBURBS* (2002); WWW.MANCHESTER2002-UK.COM

DAWSON, LES (1934–1993)

This archetypal Northern man was born in 'a cobbled street in Collyhurst', attended Cheetham Senior School, and began his career in 1947 alongside Bernard Manning in Harpurhey. He also sold vacuum cleaners in Moss Side and studied engineering at Openshaw Technical College, finally making his

name as a comedian on Hughie Green's show *Opportunity Knocks* in 1967, after which he worked regularly on television until the end of his life. His best known shows were *Blankety Blank* and *Sez Les*.
WWW.MANCHESTER2002-UK.COM

DEANSGATE

Runs from Victoria St to Chester Rd; a former 'red light district' of the city which takes its name from the lost River Dene. Deansgate is now an important part of the retail life of the city, with a number of shops and restaurants including Kendal Milne, Waterstones, Starbucks, Dimitri's, tapas bars, and also the John Rylands University Library, the Manchester Evening News building on Spinningfield, the Spanish Institute and the Great Northern Railway Warehouse offices.
☞ *See also* JOHN RYLANDS UNIVERSITY LIBRARY.

Hotel on the site of the former lying-in hospital near Deansgate.

DEBDALE PARK, GORTON

The park covers 130 acres by Gorton Reservoir and was one of Manchester's main leisure parks in Victorian and Edwardian times. The concept of public parks was devised during the middle part of the 19th century when working hours were cut to 60 hours a week. Sunday afternoon strolls in the park became a very popular pastime. Today Debdale Park has adapted to modern demands for more excitement by establishing an outdoor centre which offers water sports, power boating, windsurfing, orienteering and abseiling.
WWW.MANCHESTER2003-UK.COM

DECKER MILL

Ancoats. Cotton spinning mill built by the Murray Brothers in 1801 at right angles to Murray Mill.
ROBINA MCNEIL AND MICHAEL NEVELL, *A GUIDE TO THE INDUSTRIAL ARCHAEOLOGY OF GREATER MANCHESTER* (2000); MIKE WILLIAMS WITH D A FARNIE, *COTTON MILLS IN GREATER MANCHESTER* (1992).

DEE, DR JOHN (1527–1608)

Dr John Dee was a renowned Tudor mathematician, astronomer, astrologer and alchemist. He was warden of Chetham's College 1595–1604. This intelligent, unconventional, Cambridge-educated man, who spent much of his life searching for the Philosopher's Stone and who claimed to have discovered the elixir of life at Glastonbury Abbey, seemed an unusual choice for the post of warden. As astrologer to Queen Elizabeth I, however, and through his work in alchemy (a forerunner of chemistry often regarded as witchcraft), he had made enemies and the Queen deemed it politically desirable for him to leave London. Though he made friends with the Byron family who lived at Clayton Hall, most Mancunians were a little nervous of him and treated him with caution and respect.
☞ *See also CLAYTON HALL.*
CHAMBERS BIOGRAPHICAL DICTIONARY.

DELANEY, SHELAGH (B. 1939)

Born of Irish descent in Salford, she was educated at Pendleton High School. Her plays and novels were often classified as 'kitchen sink drama' and her best known work *A Taste of Honey* was set in 1950s Salford. She was heavily criticized for painting such an unflattering picture of Salford in decay and the grime of the dockyards, but *A Taste of Honey* was a resounding success.
WWW.MANCHESTER2002-UK.COM

DE QUINCY, THOMAS (1785–1859)

The son of a linen merchant, he was born in Market St Lane but moved to Greenheys in 1791. He was educated at Manchester Grammar School and Oxford. The encroaching millscapes were a source of depression and he wrote of the way the countryside was rapidly disappearing. De Quincy became addicted to drugs and his best known work was *Confessions of an Opium Eater*, which sold well, but he died impoverished because of his addiction.

WWW.MANCHESTER2002-UK.COM

DIDSBURY

Didsbury, a former fortified Saxon manor on the banks of the Mersey, is one of the most sought after of Manchester's suburbs. It has retained its village atmosphere and has cultivated the cafe society which is especially popular with students. A water-driven corn mill stood on the banks of the Mersey from at least 1280 until it was demolished in 1959. In medieval times common land or fields divided for use between settlements was known as 'dole' and in Didsbury the Barcicroft (barley field) and Cotton Fields were two such fields. St James's Church dates back to well before 1235, although the original wooden chapel has long since disappeared and the present building was built in 1842, extending from the stone chapel of 1620.

Adjacent to the church lies the Old Parsonage, built in the 19th century and rumoured to be haunted. Fletcher Moss, its owner, was a keen gardener and cultivated all sorts of rare and unusual plants. He gave the Parsonage Gardens to Manchester Corporation in 1914 and they are still open to the public.

Ye Olde Cock Inn, a former coaching inn, stands next door. There used to be a cock pit in the yard of the inn and the troops of Bonnie Prince Charlie are said to have stopped there for refreshment and some sport.

Pytha Fold Farm (now Paulhan Rd) had the distinction of being the landing place for the first flight from London to Manchester on 28 April 1910 for which Mr Paulhan won the sum of £10,000 from the *Daily Telegraph*.

The Towers, which housed the Shirley Institute, home of the British Cotton Industry Research Association, was built towards the end of the 19th century. On the corner of Parrs Wood Lane and School Lane, the Capitol Cinema was built in 1931, rebuilt in 1935 after a devastating fire and became the ABC Television Theatre where a number of shows were filmed for television including *Opportunity Knocks* and *Armchair Theatre*.

On Palatine Rd are the Marie Louise Gardens, presented to Didsbury by Mrs Johanne Silkenstadt in memory of her daughter Marie Louise who died tragically young shortly after her marriage in 1891.

☛ *See also* DIDSBURY HAUNTS; SWIVEL HOUSE; FLETCHER MOSS GARDENS. GLYNIS COOPER, THE ILLUSTRATED HISTORY OF THE MANCHESTER SUBURBS (2002); T F WOODALL, *A NEW HISTORY OF DIDSBURY* (1976).

DIDSBURY HAUNTS

The Old Parsonage in Didsbury, built in the 19th century, had a troubled history and servants refused to stay after complaining of mysterious noises and what they described as 'transparent wraiths floating through the trees of the graveyard and the Parsonage gardens'. The house was finally abandoned in 1850 and lay empty until it was bought by local writer and historian Fletcher Moss in 1865. He dismissed the claims, but his pet terrier dog, Gomer, seemed to have other ideas and frequently growled at the main entrance to the house with his hair and tail standing on end.

Moss seemed to think it might be an elemental spirit said to be often found close to woods and water and something that was there long before the house was built. Local villagers were far more wary and referred to the fine wrought iron gates topped by an eagle, that he acquired from the former Spread Eagle public house in Manchester and erected at the entrance to his garden, as the Gates to Hell.

The writings of Fletcher Moss are held by Central Library in St Peter's Square Manchester.

☛ *See also* DIDSBURY; SWIVEL HOUSE.

DONAT, ROBERT (1905–1958)

The star of such films as *Goodbye Mr Chips*, *The Thirty Nine Steps* and *The Inn of the Sixth Happiness* was born in Withington, the son of a Polish clerk. WWW.MANCHESTER2002-UK.COM

DUKE OF BRIDGEWATER'S CANAL

Francis, 3rd Duke of Bridgewater, built a canal from Worsley to Castlefield to carry coal from his mines to the mills of Manchester. The canal was built 1762–76 and involved several miles of underground tunnels so that the narrow-boats could reach the coal face directly to collect the coals and transport them to Manchester. James Brindley was the engineer who built this remarkable system which was regarded as the eighth wonder of the world and attracted many visitors including a Danish monarch and his court. G ASHWORTH, *THE LOST RIVERS OF MANCHESTER* (1987).

Narrow boat L S Lowry *on the Bridgewater Canal.*

DUKE'S WAREHOUSE

Castlefield. This was the warehouse of the Duke of Bridgewater. Today part of it has been converted into Dukes 92, so-called because it is right next to lock 92 on the Rochdale Canal. The clean white exterior of the pub and restaurant belie the warehouse's grimy industrial heritage.

SIMON TAYLOR ET AL., *MANCHESTER: THE WAREHOUSE LEGACY* (2002).

DYSON, JOHN, AND HIS BUTLER, COTTERILL (BOTH D. 1902)

John Dyson lived at Bradley Gate on Langley Lane in Northenden and he had a butler named Cotterill. Cotterill left his employment suddenly one day, clearly feeling aggrieved, though the reasons for this are not known. Shortly afterwards he returned with a gun and shot John Dyson dead. He was cornered in a stable behind the Church Inn and the police were called. A gun battle ensued and Cotterill himself was shot dead. Mr Dyson had been popular in Northenden and Cotterill was not. The Boer War was not long over and Cotterill was suspected of having pro-Boer sympathies, which had earned him the nickname of Kruger in the locality. The mood of the crowd which had gathered to watch turned ugly. Elbowing the police aside they dragged Cotterill's body out of the barn, kicking it along the road like a football and hurling abuse. Finally the police were able to retrieve what remained of Cotterill and he was buried hurriedly in an unmarked grave in Northenden churchyard where the police kept guard until they were sure that there would not be further reprisals.

GLYNIS COOPER, *THE ILLUSTRATED HISTORY OF THE MANCHESTER SUBURBS* (2002); DERRICK DEACON, *NORTHENDEN* (1983).

E

EASTSIDE REGENERATION

This scheme was funded in Ancoats, Miles Platting and the Northern Quarter. In Ancoats, the first urban village, mills have been reused for flats, music studios, clubs and offices. In Miles Platting there has been new housing and the conversion of Victoria Mill to flats and community facilities. In the Northern Quarter this led to a crafts centre, a Chinese arts centre, Oldham St refurbishment and Tib St artworks.

ALAN KIDD, *HISTORY OF MANCHESTER* (3RD EDN, 2002); WWW.MANCHESTER 2002-UK.COM

ECONOMIC HISTORY OF MANCHESTER

18th century

Manchester was becoming a trading centre for textiles such hosiery, silk, linen, fustian and calico. The first textile manufacturing mills were built in the 1770s and Manchester's population doubled between 1773 and 1778. Mills and manufactories, workers cottages and warehouses were being built in rapidly increasing numbers by the end of the century. The era of Cottonopolis had begun.

19th century

Manchester's golden age of textile manufacture, engineering and exports which brought wealth, prestige and prosperity to the country, but at a terrible personal price for hundreds of thousands of workers. The use of children in the mills and their working conditions were described as a 'stain on the national character'. Manchester became a city and led the world in textile

Albion Hotel, Piccadilly.

manufacture and engineering. This brought great advances and benefits in the fields of art, architecture, education, literature, science, sports and medicine; and it also spawned a social conscience and awareness out of which grew the trade union movement and the Labour Party.

20th century

A record number of sales and exports of cotton was made in 1914 on the eve of the Great War. Trade slumped after the war and never recovered. This was due to a number of factors, such as Japan, India and China undercutting prices using British textile machinery widely exported with great lack of foresight; the British manufacturers' insistence on keeping cotton prices high; the Japanese textile industry going on to 24 hour working in 1925; and the Depression of the 1930s. By the late 1960s the British cotton industry was dead.

Manchester suffered terribly. It was widely regarded as just a wet mucky place full of dark and derelict Satanic mills; but the city fought back and managed to attract more modern industries like ICI and ICL. The first computer was built in Manchester. Regeneration and redevelopment schemes were put into operation. Then in June 1996 an IRA bomb blew the heart out of the city. By a miracle no one was killed or seriously injured and it has been claimed that it was the best thing to happen to Manchester in a long time.

State of the art bridge across the River Irwell.

21st century

The city centre has been rebuilt. New business and new investment have moved in along with the glass, steel and chrome, and the 'vibrant and volatile' club and cafe scene. Manchester reinvented itself and celebrated this fact by hosting the Commonwealth Games in 2002. The eyes of the world were

'Moovin n Groovin' on the Cow Trail at Picadilly Station 2004.

turned on Manchester and liked what they found. Marketing Manchester could proudly proclaim on their advertising hoardings: 'this is not Paris/Florence/Amsterdam/ Washington ... this is Manchester'.
ALAN KIDD, *HISTORY OF MANCHESTER* (3RD EDN, 2002); WWW.SPINNINGTHE WEB.ORG.UK; GLYNIS COOPER, *HISTORY OF THE MANCHESTER SUBURBS* (2002).

EDWARD III (KING 1327–1377)

A statue of Edward III stands in a first floor niche on the outer north side of the Town Hall, commemorating Edward's contribution to Manchester's textile industry. During the 1330s he was responsible for the settlement of a

Statue of Edward III in a niche on the north side of the Town Hall facing Princess St.

number of Flemish immigrants to the Manchester area. They brought with them their weaving skills which they passed on to their English neighbours. Consequently by Tudor times Manchester had become well known for 'Manchester cottons' (a napped woollen weave) and for its 'small wares' (ribbons, garters, laces, braids, etc.). The Flemish weavers were also skilled in weaving silk and flax and this laid the foundations for the 19th-century cotton industry.
GLYNIS COOPER, *HIDDEN MANCHESTER* (2003); WWW.SPINNINGTHEWEB.ORG.UK

EMPLOYMENT
The table gives the analysis of employment in Manchester.

Public sector	26.0%
Manufacturing	17.0%
Clerical /secretarial	16.7%
Administration/management	14.1%
Other	26.2%

ALAN KIDD, *HISTORY OF MANCHESTER* (3RD EDN, 2002); WWW.MANCHESTER 2002-UK.COM

ENGELS, FRIEDRICH (1820–1895)
Born in Barmen, Germany, Engels came to Manchester in 1842, sent by his father to work for their expanding business in Market St, and rented a home at 63–65 Cecil St in Moss Side. He became interested in the Chartist Movement and in the social reforms of Robert Owen. He met Mary Burns, a young working-class Irish woman, with whom he lived until her death; then he lived with her sister Lizzie. The sisters introduced him to the working conditions of the millscapes and the wretchedness of areas like Little Ireland down by the River Medlock. He field-walked most of the inner suburbs, horrified at what he saw, describing Hulme as 'one great working man's district'. His days in Manchester were the catalyst for his writing *Conditions of the Working Classes in England* published in 1844 which has become a classic study of life in the millscapes. Engels also wrote for local newspapers including the *Manchester Guardian*, now the *Guardian*.

He met Karl Marx on a visit to Brussels in 1844. Marx visited him in Manchester in 1845 and together they worked on the *Communist Manifesto* (published in 1848, the Year of Revolutions), using the peace and seclusion of Chetham's Library for their writing and research. He also collaborated with Marx on *Das Kapital* (published in 1867). Engels and Lizzie finally left Manchester in 1870 and moved to London where he spent the remainder of his life completing, editing and translating Marx's works.
CHAMBERS BIOGRAPHICAL DICTIONARY.

ETHNIC POPULATION

Statistics extracted from the 1991 census show that 87.2% of the population are from white groups. Of the non-white population, 5.4% are from Indian/Pakistani/Bangladeshi groups, 4.7% are from black groups, 2.6% are from Chinese and other groups. 95% of West Indians and 79% of Indians live in the inner city suburbs. Moss Side has largest number of West Indian households. Longsight has largest number of Asian households.

Hulme, Cheetham and Rusholme have sizeable ethnic populations. China Town (George St/Princess St area) has a sizeable Chinese population. Ancoats has a mixed cosmopolitan population of Irish, Polish and Italian background.

ALAN KIDD, *HISTORY OF MANCHESTER* (3RD EDN, 2002).

EXCHANGE SQUARE

Shops stand on the site of the original market place and corn mill of the old town and are flanked by Marks and Spencer, Miss Selfridge and Harvey Nicholls.

WWW.MANCHESTER2002-UK.COM

EXCHANGE STATION

Hunts Bank. Immediately adjoining Victoria Station, and serving similar destinations, Exchange Station had the longest passenger platform in the world. However the station was badly damaged by bombing during the Second World War. It was closed in 1969 and demolished in the 1980s. The site is now a car park.

ALAN KIDD, *HISTORY OF MANCHESTER* (3RD EDN 2002); WWW.MANCHESTER 2002-UK.COM

F

FAIRBAIRN, WILLIAM (1789–1874)

A Scottish engineer who studied mathematics and moved to Manchester in 1817. The William Fairbairn and (until 1830s) James Lillie Ironworks branched out into iron ship building as the old wooden sailing ships began to be replaced. The firm also manufactured steam engines, water wheels, locomotives and mill gearing. In 1860 William Fairbairn won the Royal Society Gold Medal for engineering treatises.

CHAMBERS BIOGRAPHICAL DICTIONARY.

FALLOWFIELD

First mentioned in a deed of 1317, Fallowfield was still a farming area with trout streams in the 1820s. Local house names reflect this: Ashfield, The

Oaks, Mabfield, The Firs and Cabbage Hall. From the 1850s however it gradually developed as a middle-class suburb for the better off to escape the confines of the city. Alfred Waterhouse, who designed Manchester Town Hall, built his own residence, Barcombe Cottage, on Oak Drive. It eventually became a hotel but has now been demolished. Manchester Athletic Club was established on Whitworth Lane in 1891. The ground was bought by Manchester racing cyclist Reg Harris in 1955 and renamed the Harris Stadium. Subsequently Manchester University bought it and built the Owens Park complex and a car park on the site. The athletics stadium is still in use but cycling has ceased. Nearby is the Hollins Campus (for the study of domestic sciences) known locally as the 'toast rack' because of its architectural appearance.

GLYNIS COOPER, *THE ILLUSTRATED HISTORY OF THE MANCHESTER SUBURBS* (2002); PETER HELM AND GAY SUSSEX, *LOOKING BACK AT FALLOWFIELD AND RUSHOLME* (1984).

FATAL ACCIDENTS

Child labour was used extensively in the mills, partly because it was cheap and because children were smaller and more nimble than adults and could be sent underneath the machinery to clean it without the machinery needing to be stopped. Accidents of course were common. Most involved bruising, cuts and amputation of fingers; but some were much more serious. In 1844 a young lad at Quarry Bank Mill was cleaning beneath a spinning mule. It was important to be quick because the kick back from the mule as it moved back and forwards was sharp and fast. This particular day he was too slow and he was caught by the kick back. It literally smashed his head to bits and he died instantly. A few years before a little girl aged about 10 or 11 got her dress caught in moving unguarded machinery (mill owners did not see the need to waste money installing machine guards). She was whipped off her feet, whirled round and round like a rag doll, dashed against the floor and her body ripped to pieces. Despite horrific deaths like these health and safety legislation was not considered a serious issue until the latter half of the 19th century.

WWW.SPINNINGTHEWEB.ORG.UK

FAWKES, GUY, AND YE OLD SEVEN STARS INN

Guy Fawkes is described making a visit to Ye Old Seven Stars Inn by Harrison Ainsworth in his novel *Guy Fawkes*:

> after much debate, it was decided that their safest plan would be to proceed to Manchester, where Humphrey Chetham undertook to procure them safe lodgings at the Seven Stars – an excellent hostel, kept by a worthy widow,

who, he affirmed, would do anything to serve him. Accordingly, they set out at nightfall – Viviana taking her place before Guy Fawkes ... crossing Salford Bridge, they mounted Smithy Bank ... and proceeding along Cateaton St and Hanging Ditch, struck into Whithing (now Withy) Grove, at the right of which, just where a few houses were beginning to straggle up Shude Hill, stood, and still stands, the comfortable hostel of the Seven Stars. Here they stopped, and were warmly welcomed by its buxom mistress, Dame Sutcliffe. Muffled in Guy Fawkes' cloak, the priest gained the chamber, to which he was ushered unobserved. And Dame Sutcliffe, though her Protestant notions were a little scandalized at her dwelling being made the sanctuary of a Popish priest, promised, at the instance of Master Chetham, whom she knew to be no favourer of idolatry in a general way, to be answerable for his safety ... on entering the hotel, the following words will be seen on a door: 'Ye Guy Faux Chamber.' This is the room in which Guy Faux was concealed the night on which he made his escape. The old door still remains from which he made his exit.

There is also a legend that Guy Fawkes fled from troopers at Ordsall Hall via secret subterranean passages to the Seven Stars in Withy Grove. Underground passages from the hall to Manchester did exist and Guy Fawkes and his companions could have made use of them. In April 1900 a letter published in the *Manchester Guardian* stated:

I was shown a door in Hanging Bridge Hotel cellar where the arches could be seen and a door made up ... it was the entrance to an underground passage under the Irwell ... to ... Ordsall Hall ... the owner had not traversed the passage himself, but the previous owner had, but had to turn back because of bad smells ...

Manchester Notes and Queries for 1901 published the following fragment:

when the licensed house at the Cathedral end of Hanging Bridge ... was rebuilt, a tunnel was found with five or six skeletons with fragments of clothing and copper coin [dated the reign of Philip and Mary 1553–8] with Latin inscription ...

MANCHESTER NOTES AND QUERIES (1901); HARRISON AINSWORTH, *GUY FAWKES* (1837); GLYNIS COOPER, *HIDDEN MANCHESTER* (2004).

FIELDS, GRACIE (1898–1979)
Born in Rochdale she was a mill girl turned singer whose no-nonsense down-to-earth northern warmth won her many admirers. Gracie Fields was

especially popular during the 1930s and 1940s and her songs included 'Sally', 'The Biggest Aspidistra in the World', and 'Sing as We Go'. She was made a dame shortly before her death.
WWW.MANCHESTER2002-UK.COM

FINNEY, CHRIS (B. 1984)

Chris Finney, born in Marple just outside Manchester, became the youngest ever recipient of the George Cross for bravery in Iraq in 2003. He rescued a colleague from a burning tank turret; sent an SOS report from his own burning vehicle; and then, though wounded, continued to help other colleagues. He was a trooper and a Scimitar armoured vehicle driver in the Squadron of the Household Cavalry Regiment.
WWW.MANCHESTER2002-UK.COM

FIRST CHURCH OF CHRIST SCIENTIST

Daisy Bank Road. An early 20th-century church described by Professor Nikolaus Pevsner as 'one of the most original church buildings in England'. It was designed and built by architect Edgar Wood in 1903–4 and he made a few later additions. Wood was a follower of the English Art and Crafts Movement which was in total contrast to the elaborate Victorian Gothic styles. The church has pleasingly simple lines

> with a very steep gable and steeply pitched slate roof, a distinctive round turret staircase and tall chimney rising above the line of the roof to one side ... two wings stretch out diagonally on either side at the front – one was a reading room and the other a meeting hall ... another wing projects from the rear which ... contained a vestry and a boardroom.

WWW.MANCHESTER2002-UK.COM

FLETCHER MOSS GARDENS

The gardens were established by Fletcher Moss, a local writer and historian, who bought Didsbury Old Parsonage in 1865. He carefully recorded what he grew in his gardens and when he gave them to Manchester Corporation in 1914 they were renamed in his honour. Fletcher Moss wrote that his gardens contained 'a small orchid house, a rose garden and a rich and extensive collection of herbaceous plants'. There were also climbing plants which included honeysuckle, Virginia creeper and passion flowers, as well as 'cottage garden' flowers like marigolds, lilies, borage and rue.
WWW.MANCHESTER2003-UK.COM

FORMBY, GEORGE (1904–1961)

Born William Booth, the son of a Wigan music hall comedian, George Formby's trademarks were his ukulele and his cheeky Lancashire chappie persona in his songs and comedy work. Several of his early films were made in Manchester, including *Off the Dole* and *Boots! Boots!*, the latter filmed above a garage. Practically all his films were vehicles for his songs, most of which subsequently became musical hits in their own right, such as 'When I'm Cleanin' Winders' and 'With Me Little Stick of Blackpool Rock'.
WWW.MANCHESTER2002-UK.COM

FOXTROT PHANTOM

On New Years Eve 1962 most of the residents in Alderly St, Hulme, were in a cheerful frame of mind, drinking dancing and looking forward to the New Year. Then someone else joined in, knocking and banging away in a foxtrot rhythm. At first people thought it was a joker who had hidden somewhere but as the celebrations continued it soon became clear that whoever was dancing the foxtrot with such gusto was no ordinary mortal; or indeed that they were not mortal at all. For the foxtrot didn't end with New Year's Eve; it continued in one particular house every single night for six months. The knockings and bangings and thumps, always in a foxtrot rhythm, vibrated through several of the closely packed terraced houses, and inch-wide cracks began to appear in the street. Residents were terrified. Police and council officials could not trace the cause. Psychical research experts were called in but could not identify who or what was making the noise. As suddenly as it had begun it stopped, leaving residents relieved but mystified. Over forty years later there is still no explanation as to who or what the Foxtrot Phantom was.
GLYNIS COOPER, *THE ILLUSTRATED HISTORY OF THE MANCHESTER SUBURBS* (2002); CHRIS MAKEPEACE, *LOOKING BACK AT HULME, MOSS SIDE, CHORLTON-ON-MEDLOCK AND ARDWICK* (1998).

FREE TRADE HALL

Peter St. Cheap imported grain during the early 19th century led the wealthy landed gentry to lobby the ruling Tory Party to prohibit these imports and so the Corn Laws were passed in 1815. This gave home-grown corn a monopoly and prices rose so high that many people could no longer afford to buy bread. Protests grew and in 1838 the Anti Corn Law League was founded by Richard Cobden (a calico printer) and John Bright (a mill owner from Rochdale) at the York Hotel in King St. Support for the new movement grew so rapidly that a temporary wooden hall was built on Peter St to hold meetings. It became known as the Free Trade Hall. Sir Robert Peel finally repealed the Corn Laws in 1846 and Manchester became established with the principle of free trade. A stone hall replaced the wooden hall on Peter

Free Trade Hall built to commemorate the repeal of the Corn Laws.

St and was commemoratively named the Free Trade Hall. During the 20th century the hall was used for meetings and concerts, but the 21st century is witnessing its conversion to a hotel.

FRIENDS MEETING HOUSE

Mount St. The Meeting House still plays a very active part in religious and secular life. It stands opposite the back entrance of Central Library and uses its notice board to post philosophical food for thought such 'don't be afraid that your life will end, be afraid that it will never begin'. One does not necessarily have to share in Quaker beliefs to understand the sentiment. The Meeting House was built by Richard Lane in 1828 in a Classical Revival style with Greek façade and four supporting Ionic pillars. The rest of the building is in plainer brickwork. It is now a Grade II listed building.
WWW.MANCHESTER2002-UK.COM

G

GARRATT HALL

Granby Row. An imposing and picturesque black and white timbered Tudor manor house with 'numerous gables and tall chimneys', Garratt Hall, a former seat of the de Trafford family, stood on the banks of Shooter's Brook. In the late 1700s the fishpond was infilled and commemorated in the name Fishpond St, which was later subsumed by Whitworth St. The Hall itself did not survive the changes wrought by the Industrial Revolution.

During the 1730s the owner of Garratt Hall disappeared while on a business trip to London. Numerous attempts to find him failed and his wife resigned herself to his loss and settled down to bring up their children. When the eldest son came of age it became necessary to try and trace several documents that his father had with him when he disappeared and advertisements were placed in several London newspapers. A strange letter arrived advising the son to travel to London to a certain address in the Barbican. When he arrived he was blindfolded and taken some way by sedan chair to a house where a middle-aged man was waiting to meet him. It was the missing father. He explained that when he'd arrived in London all those years before he had taken lodgings with a shopkeeper and fallen passionately in love with the shopkeeper's daughter. They had married and he had gone into partnership with her father. They were very happy and he did not want details given to his family of his circumstances until after his death. The son agreed and, taking the documents, returned to the Barbican in the same manner in which he had arrived at the house. As soon as he got back to Garratt Hall, however, he told his family the whole story, though none of them ever saw the missing father again.
GLYNIS COOPER, *HIDDEN MANCHESTER* (2004); *NEWSPAPER CUTTINGS OF MANCHESTER AND SALFORD* (LANCASHIRE RECORD OFFICE, *c.*1908).

GASKELL ELIZABETH (1810–1865)

She was born in London but she was brought up in Knutsford (on which she modelled *Cranford* in 1853) after her mother's death when she was 10. Her uncle was the doctor who treated the child workers at Quarry Bank Mill and it was through accompanying him on his visits that she had her first insight of life in the mills. In 1832 she married the Unitarian minister of Cross St Chapel, the Revd William Gaskell (1805–84) and set up home at 84 Plymouth Grove in Chorlton-on-Medlock on the Longsight border. Here she raised her children and studied the working men and women of the millscapes. Horrified by what she learned, she pressed for social reforms. She used her writing to expose the appalling living and working conditions of working people in the industrial North-West and in 1848 she published her first novel *Mary Barton*. She was roundly condemned by local mill owners but she wrote *North and South* in 1855 which threw the juxtaposition of Northern millscapes and what she saw as the more civilized standards of life in Southern England into sharp relief. She and her husband were friendly with Edmund Potter and his wife, Jessie. It is said that that Edmund Potter, a tall good-looking charismatic man, was the model for John Thornton in *North and South*. Her last novel was *Wives and Daughters*, written shortly before her sudden death in 1865. In addition to her several novels she also wrote an acclaimed biography of Charlotte Bronte in 1857. Cross St Chapel holds an Elizabeth Gaskell archive which includes many of her original manuscripts, and so too does the John Rylands University Library on Deansgate.

Chambers Biographical Dictionary.

GHOST OF TOPLEY STREET

One of the houses in Topley St, Collyhurst, had been used as a spiritualists' hall until the caretakers vanished without trace. Soon afterwards, *c*.1962, a local family with young children moved into the house. One of the children, who slept in the back bedroom, complained about being woken up by 'an old man in black swinging a watch chain'. He was later joined by an elderly woman dressed in white who had 'a malicious look on her face'. Investigators from the Manchester Psychical Society were called in. They recorded tapes on which the sounds of broken glass and furniture being moved could be heard quite plainly, but nothing was actually moved or broken. Animals refused to stay in the house. The children's pet budgie was found dead. Church of England and Roman Catholic clergy tried and failed to exorcize the ghost. Finally the family had had enough. They packed their belongings and moved to Miles Platting. Who the ghosts were has never been discovered but what the clergy failed to do was eventually achieved by a bulldozer which demolished the house.

Glynis Cooper, *The Illustrated History of the Manchester Suburbs* (2002); Allan D Barlow, *A History of Collyhurst and Harpurhey* (1977).

GIANT CUCUMBER

In 1797 Robert Tinkler was proprietor of the Grapes and Compass Coffee House and Tea Gardens in Collyhurst. As well as refreshing themselves his customers could walk in the gardens and dance to brass bands which played there. He grew fruit, vegetables and flowers. In the summer of 1814 one of his cucumbers grew to an unprecedented 7ft 8ins (2.3m) in length. People came from far and wide to see it. London got to hear of this amazing feat of nature and he was asked to cut it and send it to the Prince Regent (later George IV) for royal inspection. This he did but sadly it is not on record as to whether His Royal Highness kept the cucumber for his own cucumber sandwiches or whether he returned it to the Tea Gardens.

GLYNIS COOPER, *THE ILLUSTRATED HISTORY OF THE MANCHESTER SUBURBS* (2002); ALLAN D BARLOW, *A HISTORY OF COLLYHURST AND HARPURHEY* (1977).

GMEX

By the mid-1980s Central Station had been refurbished at a cost of £20million to become one of the country's largest exhibition centres covering 10,000 square metres. The 'vast vaulted roof' is said to be held up by 'sheer engineering ingenuity and simple geometry'. Exhibitions, fairs and performances are held regularly; and Torvill and Dean staged an ice spectacular there.

☛ *See also* **CENTRAL STATION**.

ALAN KIDD, *HISTORY OF MANCHESTER* (3RD EDN, 2002); WWW.MANCHESTER 2002-UK.COM

GMEX, formerly Central Station.

GORTON

The name literally means dirty town and there have been times when Gorton has lived up to this description. It stands by the Gore Brook on whose banks there was a corn mill in the 14th century. Those who had their corn ground there were informed they 'ought to grind to the sixteenth grain', which seems to have been a means of ensuring some grain would be left for the miller as payment.

Debdale Park in Gorton is still a pretty place to walk and this has been a popular pastime there for over a hundred years. Modern tastes are more demanding so the park now offers power boating activities, windsurfing, orienteering and abseiling.

The Ashton Canal passes through Gorton and with the canal came the Gorton Mills built in 1852. Two years later the Beyer Peacock Railway Works began production at Gorton Foundry. The company manufactured and serviced railway rolling stock and built more than 8,000 locomotives for shipment all over the world. The steam locomotives were internationally renowned for quality, safety and reliability; and waited in long rows at the dockside of the Manchester Ship Canal for transportation. Also situated in Gorton were the Crossley Works which made trucks and buses.

In 1861 the building of St Francis Monastery began in the unlikely setting of Gorton Lane. Hand-built by the monks of the Franciscan Order from local bricks and whatever else they could find, it was completed in 1867. The monastic church was designed by Edward Pugin and was finished in 1872. Following gifts of a stained-glass altar window, lady chapel, a sanctuary lamp, wrought iron communion railing, font and pulpit, the church was finally completed in 1885 when the high altar was installed. The monastery has survived and is currently undergoing restoration work under the Angels Regeneration scheme.

In 1942, almost opposite St Francis Monastery, Myra Hindley was born. She and her partner, Ian Brady, tortured and murdered a number of children from the Gorton area in the mid-1960s and then buried them on the lonely Saddleworth Moors. The case became known as the Moors Murders and she and Brady were caught and sentenced to life imprisonment. Myra Hindley died in prison in 2002.

☛ *See also St Francis Monastery; Moors Murders.*

Glynis Cooper, *The Illustrated History of the Manchester Suburbs* (2002).

GRANADA TELEVISION

Granada Television is situated on Quay St and the building stands over the culverted Manchester and Salford Junction Canal. Granada Television began in 1956 and its headquarters is at the Albert Dock in Liverpool. It produces

Granada Television on Quay St.

news and regional affairs programmes, *Good Morning*, weather, sport and a number of programmes which are networked, such as *Costa del Cabaret*, *The Way We Were*, dramas and history programmes. Visitors can go on studio tours to see sets used on well-known programmes, notably *Coronation Street*. WWW.GRANADATV.COM

GREATER MANCHESTER COUNTY RECORD OFFICE
Marshall St, New Cross. Hidden in an old textile warehouse on the edge of Ancoats, the GMCRO holds a wide range of maps and archives, and photographs used to promote the Cotton Board in the 1950s and 1960s. WWW.GMCRO.CO.UK

GREAT NORTHERN RAILWAY COMPANY GOODS WAREHOUSE
Built in 1898 on Watson St it towers over Peter St and Deansgate. Trains arrived from Central Station (now the GMEX) and 'goods were raised and

lowered using hydraulic power onto a specially constructed iron viaduct alongside the line'. A tunnel ran beneath the warehouse, connecting to the Manchester and Salford Canal junction. Today the warehouse has shops, cafes, offices and a car park.
SIMON TAYLOR ET AL., *MANCHESTER: THE WAREHOUSE LEGACY* (2002); WWW.MANCHESTER2002-UK.COM

GREEN ROOM
Off Oxford Rd. Tucked away in a converted railway arch beneath Oxford Rd station, on the edge of what would have been the slum of Little Ireland in the 1840s, the Green Room is an experimental theatre established in 1983 to perform marginal and 'difficult' plays. The theatre offers a centre for artistic activity and has been involved in Manchester festivals including 'Queer Up North', Manchester International Arts, and Manchester Poetry Festival, the Commonwealth Film Festival and the Manchester Jazz Festival.
WWW.GREENROOMARTS.ORG/

GREENWOOD, WALTER (1903–1974)
This very Northern writer was born in Salford and educated at Langworthy Road Council School. Most of his reading and studying was done in Salford Library and his letters and manuscripts are deposited with Salford University. He wrote a number of novels but he is best remembered for *Love on the Dole*, written during the Depression of the 1930s.
WWW.MANCHESTER2002-UK.COM

GROCER'S WAREHOUSE
Castlefield. In the early 1770s this warehouse was built beside the coal wharf. It was five storeys high and had five window bays facing the canal and a single entrance two storeys high. Boats entered here for unloading at the internal dock where there was a water-powered hoist. In 1793 the warehouse was extended and doubled in length. The warehouse was demolished in 1960 but it is commemorated by a giant rusting cog wheel bearing the following inscription:

> Built on the site where coal was first brought to Manchester by canal for the 1st Duke of Bridgewater. The warehouse marks the location where coal was transferred to street level using water wheel driven machinery designed and built, by James Brindley. The delivery of cheap coal marked the beginning of the Industrial revolution and helped establish Manchester as a principal manufacturing centre.
>
> As a result of increasing trade and success of the scheme a warehouse for the storage of provisions was constructed on the site of the coal wharf.

Site of former Grocer's Warehouse at Castlefield. Transcription of text on plaque under Castlefield.

The original building was demolished in 1960 and the partial reconstruction which incorporated a water wheel driven hoist was completed in 1967.

GLYNIS COOPER, *HIDDEN MANCHESTER* (2004); SIMON TAYLOR ET AL., *MANCHESTER: THE WAREHOUSE LEGACY* (2002).

GUNPOWDER PLOT AT ORDSALL HALL

The 14th-century Ordsall Hall in Salford, barely a mile from the Manchester boundary, is said to have been the setting for the hatching of the Gunpowder Plot by Guy Fawkes and his accomplices. Leading off the Great Hall is the Star Chamber, so-called because of the lead stars on the ceiling placed there by an early Tudor craftsman. In the words of Frank Hird, there is an 'old wide chimney-piece, and in the right hand corner a small door that once opened upon a secret passage leading to a staircase in the chimney, which communicated with a little chapel, and hiding places in the roof'.

It was here in the Star Chamber, according to the popular legend immortalized in Harrison Ainsworth's novel *Guy Fawkes*, that Robert Catesby and Guy Fawkes hatched the Gunpowder Plot in 1605. Although never proved, it is entirely possible. The Radclyffes were a Catholic family (and heavily fined for it) and acquaintances of Catesby's family who were prominent Northamptonshire Catholics. Catesby was in deep trouble, having been involved in a rebellion led by the Earl of Essex against Queen Elizabeth I and he had also been accused of trying to poison the Queen; both treasonable acts. Life was uncomfortable and dangerous for him in London and Ordsall Hall offered him sanctuary at a safe distance. There is often a grain of truth in folklore and it is probable that Guy Fawkes did indeed stay at Ordsall Hall. There is no evidence that Sir John Radclyffe, who owned the hall at the time, knew anything of the Gunpowder Plot, and little reason why he should have known of any desperate whisperings that took place in the Star Chamber.

In Harrison Ainsworth's novel, Guy Fawkes also fell in love with Viviana Radclyffe who was later tortured to try and make her reveal the secrets of the Gunpowder Plot. There was no member of the Radclyffe family named Viviana, however, and the Gunpowder Plot was discovered in London. The only contemporary Radclyffe women at Ordsall were Margaret, who had died in 1599, and Jane, aged around 30 in 1605, who was married to Sir Ralph Constable.

MANCHESTER NOTES AND QUERIES (1901); HARRISON AINSWORTH, *GUY FAWKES* (1837); FRANK HIRD, *LANCASHIRE STORIES* (1913); GLYNIS COOPER, *HIDDEN MANCHESTER* (2004).

H

HALLÉ, SIR CHARLES (1819–1895)

Charles Hallé was born in Hagen, Westphalia. He became a talented pianist and a respected conductor who moved to Paris where he became friendly with composers and performers such as Chopin, Liszt, Berlioz and Wagner. The Year of Revolutions in 1848 forced him to move to England and he settled in Manchester because it had a sizeable German population. He lived in Greenheys Lane teaching the piano and trying to improve standards in conducting music. In 1857 he formed the Hallé Orchestra. He also helped to found the Royal College of Music in Manchester from where he selected talented musicians for his orchestra.

CHAMBERS BIOGRAPHICAL DICTIONARY.

HANGING BRIDGE

For over two hundred years the only clue to Hanging Bridge was the name, but during demolition work near the Cathedral in the 1880s astonished labourers found part of the arch of a bridge several feet below ground. The City Surveyors Department then supervised a careful excavation of the site. Slowly a double-arched stone bridge emerged. The bridge was 36 yards (just over 30m) long and 3 yards (2.75m) wide. It had been surmised from the name that the bridge had been a small rope bridge strung over a stream but this was a very solid well-built structure capable of carrying a good volume of traffic. Part of the bridge was of an earlier date than the rest, including the buttress of the southern arch, and there were indications that this might have been the foundations of a drawbridge, hence the name Hanging Bridge.

In 1937, however, the bridge was said to have taken its name from the open space at the Cateaton St end of the bridge (close to the present positions of Sinclairs Oyster Bar and the Old Wellington Inn) where public executions took place. The most likely explanation is likely to be of a more natural origin. There are references to the Hengand Brigge in 1343 which crossed a deep ditch through which a swiftly flowing stream descended from the River Irk to the River Irwell. This ditch was 120ft (37m) wide and 40ft (12.3m) deep by the time it reached the Irwell and the stream was considered to have been the lost River Dene from which Deansgate takes its name. Hen is an old English word for wild birds such as moorhens and waterhens while gan derives from a Welsh word meaning 'situated between two hills'.

In 1343 Manchester was little more than a village surrounded by open countryside across which numerous streams and rivers flowed. The main settlement was on the sandstone outcrop on which the cathedral stands, and the market place which lay just to the south (on the site currently occupied by Marks and Spencer), linked by a bridge across a rushing stream deep in its valley (which became known as Hanging Ditch). Hanging Bridge is mentioned in the Court Leet (magistrates) records of 1343 stating that 'dyvers persons drove oxen across it and through the grave yard for a short cut'. By 1600 Hanging Ditch was condemned as an open sewer and in 1682 it disappears from the records. In 1772 *Raffald's Directory* records nine houses built along the line of the bridge and it is certain that by 1800 both the ditch and the bridge had been culverted: the bridge probably during the first phase of town planning in the early 1770s, the ditch probably earlier as it had become a health hazard.

Today the ditch is dry and remains mostly culverted beneath the buildings of 19th-century Cottonopolis. Hanging Bridge has been preserved as a feature of the coffee shop in the basement of the Cathedral bookshop. It is actually possible to sit at a table in the old riverbed by the northern arch and

Medieval 'Hanging Bridge' built of stone near Manchester Cathedral, partly hidden by modern buildings; today forms part of a coffee shop.

drink coffee – well worth a visit for the fine example of medieval bridge architecture matched by the equally fine cappuccino.
WWW.ART.MAN.AC.UK/FIELDARCHAEOLOGY CENTRE/

HARPURHEY

Harpurhey used to be 'very pretty countryside ... where the river Irk ... a clear stream full of fish, ran through woodlands full of wild hyacinths and meadows of daffodils and primroses', which lay to the west of Kersal Moor where the Manchester races used to take place. There was a cottage dyeing industry for centuries in the area and when, in 1812, Harpurhey was sold to the Andrew family who worked in the dyeing trade, the area started to become industrial. Andrews Dye Works became successful in the production of 'Turkey Red', which didn't run like the old madder reds, and also for a new fainter coloured print of lilac. Turkey Lane was so named as it led down to the Turkey Red dye works near Moss Brook.

In 1836, Robina Andrew gave land for the building of Christ Church and money was raised from all quarters, including a helping hand from Queen Adelaide, wife of William IV. The church was completed in 1837; but it was decided that a separate cemetery should be built for burials from all denominations; and to serve a wider area. The Manchester General Cemetery, bounded by Queens Park, Hendham Vale, the Manchester and Rochdale roads, opened in 1837. Queens Park was one of the first two public parks to open in Manchester in 1846 as a response to the increased leisure hours of the cotton workers.

☛ *See also MANCHESTER MUMMY.*

GLYNIS COOPER, *THE ILLUSTRATED HISTORY OF THE MANCHESTER SUBURBS* (2002). ALLAN D BARLOW, *A HISTORY OF COLLYHURST AND HARPURHEY* (1977).

HAY, WILL (1889–1949)

Best known for his characterization of an eccentric school teacher, based on stories told to him by his sister who was a school teacher in Cheetham Hill. Will Hay began his working life as an engineering apprentice at his father's Manchester company, though he later became an interpreter for the Calico Printers' Association. He also learned how to fly and was a keen astronomer. Hay acted for a year at Manchester's Palace Theatre where he met Fred Karno's Army Troupe. He appeared with them in a number of films during the 1930s and 1940s such as *Boys will be Boys, Where there's a Will* and *The Goose Steps Out*.

WWW.MANCHESTER2002-UK.COM

HEATON HALL

Heaton Park, Blackley. Heaton Hall was originally built by the Egerton family during the late 1600s but it was redesigned and rebuilt by the architect James Wyatt after Sir Thomas Egerton married heiress Eleanor Assheton in 1772. An Italian artist, Biagio Rebecca, painted the decorative work and the pictures and the Pompeiian Cupola Room. The furniture and mahogany doors came from Gillows of Lancaster. In 1820 Lewis Wyatt remodelled the library and added the Orangery. Today the Hall is a Grade I listed building because of the excellence of its neoclassical design. Guests as diverse as the Duke of Wellington, Benjamin Disraeli and the actress Fanny Kemble stayed here during the 19th century; so too did General Tom Thumb, an American dwarf who stood just 31ins (32.5cm) high.

☛ *See also HEATON PARK.*

GLYNIS COOPER, *THE ILLUSTRATED HISTORY OF THE MANCHESTER SUBURBS* (2002); WWW.GMCRO.CO.UK

Frontage of Manchester's first town hall which stood on King Street and was demolished c.1912.
It still stands today in Heaton Park.

HEATON PARK

Blackley. Heaton Park lies in the grounds of Heaton Hall, the 17th-century
seat of the Egerton family. The park covers 640 acres, making it Manchester's
largest public park. Heaton Park Races were run here during the 19th century.
The large boating lake is fronted by the Greek inspired façade of Manchester's
first Town Hall, which stood in King St and was demolished in 1912. Nearby
stands a huge rock known as the Papal Monument. The Orangery at the Hall
is now a restaurant and conference centre and there is a farm which breeds
Highland cattle, Soay sheep, peacocks and waterfowl. The pitch and putt golf
course stands on the site of a mock-up of the battlefield trenches used for
training soldiers during the Great War (1914–18).
☛ *See also HEATON HALL.*
WWW.MANCHESTER2003-UK.COM

HIDDEN GEM

St Mary's Church, Mulberry St. St Mary's was built in 1794, the year after
the Act of Religious Toleration had finally been passed which allowed

Catholics to worship openly once again. This makes the church 'the oldest post-Reformation Catholic church founded as a church in any major centre of population in England'. The church was built on Mulberry St, so-called because of the large mulberry tree which flourished there on land which until the mid-1700s had been meadow and pasture. The tree has long gone and Mulberry St is now a back street hidden from sight by the buildings of Deansgate, John Dalton St, Albert Square and Brazennose St.

The present church only dates from 1848 and was designed by Weightman and Hadfield. The interior of the church is clean and white with marble support pillars and the central dome has eight pairs of beautiful stained-glass windows. The highlight is the Norman Adams paintings of the Stations of the Cross, savagely colourful and impressive paintings which are nationally important works of art. Despite this, the church has a feeling of great peace and people come to pray, to admire the works of art or simply to escape for a few minutes from the frantic 21st century world outside.

St Mary's was painted in a winter setting by L S Lowry in 1962 as *The Hidden Gem in the Snow*. He captured the essence of the hidden church, snuggled in a back street yet still a community focus.

GLYNIS COOPER, *HIDDEN MANCHESTER* (2004); WWW.MANCHESTER2002-UK.COM

HILL, ALBERT (1895–1971)

Albert Hill was born in Hulme, one of ten children. He worked first in a cotton mill and then for a hat manufacturer. He served in the 10th Battalion of the Royal Welsh Fusiliers during the First World War and served in France and Flanders. He was awarded the Victoria Cross for gallantry and bravery at the Battle of the Somme and he also won the Croix de Guerre.

WWW.MANCHESTER2002-UK.COM

HOUGH HALL

Moston. The hall stood on Hough Hall Lane behind Moston Lane School. It was a Tudor farmhouse, built by the Asshetons of Middleton and sold to the Hough family in 1613. The Houghs were Royalists and during the Civil War (1640–9) the hall was temporarily confiscated. Afterwards it was sold to James Lightbowne and then passed through marriage to the Minshull and the Aytoun families before being sold again to Samuel Taylor in the 1770s. He built Moston House on the site. This was taken over in 1886 by the Daughters of the Cross, a religious house from Liège, who established a home for thirty orphan girls. The Margaret Ashton Sixth Form College stands on the site today.

GLYNIS COOPER, *THE ILLUSTRATED HISTORY OF THE MANCHESTER SUBURBS* (2002); BRIAN SEARLE, *MOSTON STORY* (1983).

HULME

Hulme took its name from the Danish word for a small island, which it may well have been in Viking times, bounded as it is on three sides by water: that of the Rivers Irwell, Medlock and Cornbrook. Hulme Hall stood on the banks of the Irwell and dated back to the 13th century. The hall was demolished in 1845, but there were legends attached to it of 'unearthly demons' guarding buried treasure and treasure seekers scoured the surrounding land until well into the 19th century.

Hulme grew into one of the grimmest of the central millscape suburbs. In 1801 its population was just 1,677. Thirty years later it had grown to 26,982; then in the next ten years it almost tripled to about 78,000; and doubled again between 1841 and 1851 to 156,000. In 1844 Hulme was described by Friedrich Engels as 'one great working people's district'. Small worker's cottages were built around courts or small squares which had washing and sanitation facilities in the centre. Frequently insufficient facilities were provided and there are horror stories of 300 people sharing a single toilet. Poorer families lived together in just one room. Cellar dwellers often found their homes soaked with untreated effluent which had seeped through the floors from the inadequate sewerage and drainage systems.

The most remarkable industrial creation to come out of Hulme was the Rolls Royce motor car. In 1904 Henry Royce, an electrical engineer, and Charles Rolls, a car salesman, met at the Midland Hotel in Manchester and formed a partnership. The first Rolls Royce was produced in 1905 and by 1906 the company had established their works in Cooke St. Hulme suffered badly during the Blitz in the Second World War and by the 1960s large-scale slum clearance resulted in the building of crescent shaped blocks of flats known as the Hulme Crescents. The flats proved a social disaster and were demolished in the early 1990s. St George's is now the centre of a redevelopment area and the church itself has been converted into upmarket apartments.

☛ *See also* HULME HALL.

GLYNIS COOPER, *THE ILLUSTRATED HISTORY OF THE MANCHESTER SUBURBS* (2002); CHRIS MAKEPEACE, *LOOKING BACK AT HULME, MOSS SIDE, CHORLTON-ON-MEDLOCK AND ARDWICK* (1998).

HULME HALL

Hulme Hall stood close to a bend in the River Irwell. It was a picturesque black and white timbered building which fell victim to the Industrial Revolution when it was demolished in 1845 to make way for the Cheshire Lines railway. Today the Metrolink thunders past above the site. The Hall's owners included Sir Thomas Prestwich, Lady Ann Bland (who built St Ann's Church), and the Duke of Bridgewater.

The Prestwich family owned the hall from the 1300s to the 1660s. It was lost to the family by Sir Thomas Prestwich who borrowed too heavily during the Civil War to aid the Royalist cause on the promise that his mother had hidden valuable treasure in the grounds. Unfortunately for Sir Thomas his mother had a seizure which rendered her dumb and immobile and she died without revealing the whereabouts of her treasure. In victory the Parliamentarians under Cromwell vented their anger on Sir Thomas for supporting the king. He was heavily fined and parts of his estate were confiscated. Impoverished he mortgaged the Hall to Sir Nicholas Mosley, who finally bought it outright in 1673, and Sir Thomas died in great poverty.

During the 18th and 19th centuries, the tales of the buried treasure became well known. Unscrupulous fortune tellers would cheat the unwary and the desperate out of their money by claiming to know where the treasure

Site of Hulme Hall where 'unearthly demons' are said to guard buried treasure.

lay buried. The Duke of Bridgewater, who purchased the hall in 1764 but never lived there, was well aware of these tales but did nothing to stop the fortune hunters who trod his land. By 1845 the hall was in a dilapidated condition. Just before its demolition, several panels of grotesque wooden figures were removed from the hall and taken to Worsley Hall. They were said to be likenesses of the 'unearthly demons' that Thomas Prestwich's mother had conjured to guard her treasure. There is an engraving of Hulme Hall shortly before its demolition showing a full moon glowing on the waters of the Irwell and the smoking chimneys of Manchester in the distance. It is a haunting image and difficult to reconcile with the grim surroundings of the former site of the hall today.

GLYNIS COOPER, *HIDDEN MANCHESTER* (2002) AND *THE ILLUSTRATED HISTORY OF THE MANCHESTER SUBURBS* (2002).

HULME REGENERATION LTD 1992

The Hulme Crescent flats, intended to replace former slum dwellings, were demolished in the 1990s. This rebuilding programme converted some of the older buildings, including St George's Church, to flats and apartments; while others were built in warehouse style blocks in keeping with the locality and the canal side.

ALAN KIDD, *HISTORY OF MANCHESTER* (3RD EDN, 2002); WWW.MANCHESTER 2002-UK.COM

HUSKISSON, WILLIAM

At the opening of the Manchester-Liverpool Railway in 1830 there was a tragic accident and Mr William Huskisson MP and President of the Board of Trade was run over by a train. He had stumbled from a carriage on an embankment, where there was only room to stand between the two sets of railway lines, panicked, and fell in front of an oncoming train. He received severe leg injuries and was carried to the vicarage in Eccles where, despite devoted nursing by the vicar's wife, he died five days later.

WWW.MSIM.ORG.UK

I

ICE CREAM MANUFACTURE

During the 1880s the Italian community in Ancoats utilized part of the Ice Plant Building (built *c.*1860 with an attached ice-making plant to store fruit, fish and vegetables) to make ice cream Subsequently about seventy ice cream barrow businesses were founded in Ancoats cottages and these included the Granelli business.

WWW.SPINNINGTHEWEB.ORG.UK

IMPERIAL CHEMICAL INDUSTRIES

The company had a large works in Crumpsall close to Springfield Hospital. Crumpsall lies on the edge of the traditional northern suburbs where dyeing and bleaching were carried out. ICI provided much needed employment in the area as the textile industry declined.

GLYNIS COOPER, *ILLUSTRATED HISTORY OF THE MANCHESTER SUBURBS* (2002).

IMPERIAL WAR MUSEUM NORTH

The museum, which is part of the Lowry complex in Salford, offers an unusual and unique insight into the meaning of war. The building is designed as three shards of a shattered globe, representing air, earth and water, symbolizing the way in which war devastates the world. The Land Shard is the largest and has six war 'time-lines' (1900–14, 1914–18, 1919–38, 1939–45, 1946–90, 1990–present), plus half a dozen special exhibitions featuring different aspects of war.

The showpieces of the museum are its three 'Big Picture Shows' entitled 'Why War?', 'Weapons of War', and 'Children and War', during which 'over sixty projectors throw images onto twenty screens, some of them five metres high'. The result is that visitors suddenly find themselves surrounded by war with all its drama, fear, tragedy and destruction. In a dim half light, images of bombed streets and houses, rescuers clawing at rubble, fields of poppies, children in gas masks, flash on to the walls; and the noise of whining sirens, gunfire, explosions and fighter planes overhead drowns the reality of peaceful, normal everyday life. It is an emotional and sobering experience during which the audience sees, hears and learns more about war during fifteen minutes than most of them will experience in a lifetime.

The Imperial War Museum North proclaims that it is 'a war museum with a heart' and it is impossible to remain unmoved or indifferent to the way in which it portrays the reality of war. Entrance is free and the nearest Metrolink stop is Harbour City on the Eccles line.

WWW.IWM.ORG.UK

INDIA HOUSE

Whitworth St. Huge former textile warehouse taking up a considerable length of the street.

SIMON TAYLOR ET AL., *MANCHESTER: THE WAREHOUSE LEGACY* (2002).

ISHERWOOD, LAWRENCE (1917–1989)

He was born in Wigan in Greater Manchester and educated locally. Isherwood was a contemporary of L S Lowry and, like him, painted northern industrial landscapes, winning the accolade from one critic of 'being among the best English painters of our time'. During the 1960s he gained a wider

audience through his unconventional and often controversial paintings of celebrities. He rarely sold his paintings but relented when the Prince of Wales asked to buy one. His work is now exhibited around the world.
WWW.MANCHESTER2002-UK.COM

J

JACKSON, JOHN (D. 1888)

A plumber from Leeds and a heavy drinker. At one point he had joined the army but he had been convicted of horse stealing and was discharged in 1885. He moved to Manchester and began a career in burglary. He was caught and sentenced to six months in Strangeways Prison. While he was there the prison matron discovered a gas leak in her home and it was agreed that, because of his plumbing skills, he should be escorted by a warder to her house to repair the leak. John Jackson, in the custody of a warder named Webb, was taken to the house to effect the repair. When he had completed his work he attacked Webb with a hammer, fracturing his skull, stole the warder's boots and escaped from the house by removing slates from the attic roof. He survived on the run by stealing and house breaking before finally being recaptured in June 1888. He finally confessed to killing the warder and was executed by hangman James Berry later that summer.
WWW.MANCHESTER2002-UK.COM

JERSEY STREET NEW MILL

Ancoats. Cotton spinning mill built in 1804 by Murray brothers to form three sides of a courtyard with the Murray Mill and Decker Mill.
ROBINA MCNEIL AND MICHAEL NEVELL, *A GUIDE TO THE INDUSTRIAL ARCHAEOLOGY OF GREATER MANCHESTER* (2000); MIKE WILLIAMS WITH D A FARNIE, *COTTON MILLS IN GREATER MANCHESTER* (1992).

JEWISH MUSEUM

This unique museum is located in the former Spanish and Portuguese Synagogue on Cheetham Hill Rd. The Synagogue was built in Moorish fashion for Sephardi (Mediterranean) Jews in 1874. It closed in 1982 due to a population shift and reopened in 1984. The ground floor has been preserved as a testament to Jewish worship while the first floor ladies gallery has been converted to a museum of Jewish life and includes a table set for the Sabbath meal, a waterproof garment maker's workshop and the office of Joseph Massel, together with documentary and photographic displays.

The ground floor remains largely unchanged from the 19th century. It is dominated by the Ark, a satin-lined cupboard below a circular stained-glass window depicting Jewish religious symbols. Below the window and above the

Ark burns an Everlasting Light as in the Temple of Jerusalem. Within the Ark are kept the Torah Scrolls (rolls of parchment wound on wooden rods on which the five books of Moses have been handwritten) and each year they are read from start to finish.

The Jewish Sabbath is on Saturday and so the museum is open Sunday-Thursday and, by appointment only, on Fridays.
WWW.MANCHESTERJEWISHMUSEUM.COM

JOHN LEWIS PARTNERSHIP, EX PICCADILLY
For almost a century the John Lewis Partnership store was an essential part of Piccadilly. It stood on the site where T K Maxx, Primark and MacDonalds now have their retail outlets. Like Kendal Milne, Lewis's combined production with retail and at one time 300 tailors and boot and shoe makers were employed by Lewis's based on Piccadilly.
WWW.MANCHESTER2002-UK.COM

JOHN RYLANDS UNIVERSITY LIBRARY
Deansgate. The library is a tribute by his widow, Enriqueta, to John Rylands, 'Manchester's most successful cotton magnate' who died in 1888. It is a neo-Gothic confection in grey and rose pink Cumbrian sandstone, with fixtures and fittings of Polish oak, which was designed by Basil Champneys and took nine years to complete. The Reading Room was built at first-floor level to minimize traffic noise. There are stained-glass windows and statues of John and Enriqueta Rylands at either end of the tall vaulted room with its polished bookcases and study desks hidden in discreet alcoves. Twenty statues represent the fields of religion, literature, science and printing, reflecting Mrs Rylands's desire for art, science and Nonconformist theology to dominate her collections.

Enriqueta Rylands died in 1908 but her endowments meant that by the 1920s the Library already owned 125,000 books and 9,000 manuscripts. Today the Library has amassed priceless items and collections including 4,000 'incunabula' (books printed before 1501), a copy of the Gutenberg Bible, Caxton's *Canterbury Tales*, Shakespeare texts, Chinese, Japanese and Jewish literature, the scientific papers of John Dalton and Sir Bernard Lovell.
☛ *See also* JOHN DALTON; BERNARD LOVELL.
WWW.MANCHESTER.LIBRARY.AC.UK

JOHN RYLANDS WAREHOUSE
Piccadilly. John Rylands's merchanting warehouse is a plain white five-storey building which stands out from the more decorative grey stone warehouses. It was built in 1930 of Portland Stone on the corner of Tib St and Piccadilly and is today home to Debenham's department store.
SIMON TAYLOR ET AL., *MANCHESTER: THE WAREHOUSE LEGACY* (2002).

Joshua Hoyle's warehouse, now the Malmaison Hotel. Doll's hospital used to be in right-hand wing.

JOSHUA HOYLE & SON

London Rd. A steel-framed warehouse built close to Piccadilly Station Approach and alongside the Rochdale Canal in 1904 by Charles Heathcote. After the end of Cottonopolis, the warehouse fell into disuse. For a while, during the 1970s, there was a Doll's Hospital in the end wing furthest from Station Approach. The warehouse has now been refurbished and reutilized as the Malmaison Hotel, with an emphasis on French decor, cuisine and comfort, and luxury bedrooms have replaced the former Doll's Hospital.

GLYNIS COOPER, *HIDDEN MANCHESTER* (2004); SIMON TAYLOR ET AL., *MANCHESTER: THE WAREHOUSE LEGACY* (2002).

JOULE, JAMES PRESCOTT (1818–1889)

James Joule was born at New Bailey St in Salford, the son of a local brewer. John Dalton taught him mathematics and algebra and he won a prize for his first experiments in electro-magnetism. By 1840 Joule had a laboratory at Pendlebury, where he studied units of force and their effect on heat and formulated the theory of heat dynamics – that heat is produced when force is applied. He defined the unit of energy now named after him as the joule or J.

For this work he was awarded the Royal Medal of the Royal Society in 1852, and in 1860 he was elected President of the Literary and Philosophical Society. Joule was made President of the British Association in 1872. He was also a keen painter and photographer.
WWW.MANCHESTER2002-UK.COM

K

KAY, LOUISA (19TH CENTURY)

She was born in Lancashire and moved to Manchester on her marriage to Sidney Potter, the brother of Edmund Potter, spending the rest of her life there. In 1877 she wrote *Lancashire Memories*, a book of her childhood, evoking memories of a still rural Lancashire in the early 19th century before the millscapes altered the landscapes forever; describing her childish pleasures, playing in the stream with her cousins, going harvesting and buying sweetmeats and trinkets from a girl with her hair in paper curlers. GLYNIS REEVE, *A NORTH COUNTRY LASS* ... (2001).

KELLY, HENRY (1887–1960)

Henry Kelly was an Irish Catholic born in Collyhurst. He became a Sergeant Major in the Manchester Regiment and was awarded the Victoria Cross for service on the Somme in 1915. Later he was awarded the Military Cross for service in Italy. By 1918 he had been wounded twice and promoted to major. After the war he and his brothers opened grocery shops on Rochdale Rd and Upper Chorlton Rd. Subsequently he worked as a landlord for a number of Manchester pubs. Henry Kelly also fought in the International Brigades against the fascists in the Spanish Civil War during the late 1930s.He died at Prestwich in 1960.
WWW.MANCHESTER2002-UK.COM

KENDAL MILNE

Kendal Milne have operated their Deansgate store for over 150 years. They bought the building from S & J Watts, who had been using it as a warehouse, when Watts moved to their new premises on Portland St, now the Britannia Hotel. Originally there were three founder members, Kendal, Milne and Faulkner, who began working together in the 1830s, and they called their new store The Bazaar. It was a forerunner of the modern department store. The store is still popular today and has been termed Manchester's answer to

Harrods. However their tenure has not been without drama. In 1872 a story was headlined in the local newspapers 'Horse-whipped at Kendals'. The article continued

> a male assistant in the drapery department was busy serving customers when a girl arrived, in a violent temper, and thrashed him soundly ... it appeared that he had jilted her and then he had circulated a scandalous report about her ...

WWW.MANCHESTERONLINE.CO.UK

KHAN, AMIR (B. 1986)

Born in Bury, educated in Bolton, Amir Khan trained as a lightweight boxer. In 2004 he won the gold medal at the European Championships in Lithuania and in April that same year qualified in Bulgaria for the Athens Olympics. He won the world junior lightweight crown in Korea in June 2004. At all three events he won the best boxer award. Khan was Britain's only boxing entry at the Olympics and he won the silver medal in the lightweight boxing division, becoming the youngest Briton ever to win an Olympic medal for boxing.

WWW.MANCHESTER2002-UK.COM

KILBURN, PROFESSOR TOM, CBE (1922–2001)

A Cambridge graduate who, with Freddie Williams, was responsible for 'the design and development of the first so-called Baby Computer capable of stored memory' at Manchester University in the 1950s. They discovered how to store information in digital form on a cathode ray tube which became known as the 'Williams Tube'. This was developed as the Ferranti Mark 1 Computer in 1951, a 'forerunner of modern digital computers'. Atlas, a more powerful machine, followed in 1962. Manchester University established the country's first Department of Computer Science under Tom Kilburn.

WWW.MANCHESTER2002-UK.COM

KING STREET

King St, in two parts, East and West, runs from Spring Gardens to Deansgate and Deansgate to St Mary's Parsonage. It was formerly the civic centre where the first Town Hall stood and it is now an area of designer label shopping with names such as Armani, Jaeger, FCUK, Vivienne Westwood, Hobbs, Karen Millen and Jigsaw.

WWW.MANCHESTER2002-UK.COM

KINGSLEY, SIR BEN (B. 1943)

Born Krishna Banji he attended Manchester Grammar School. He turned down a recording contract with the former Beatles manager, Brian Epstein, to join *Coronation Street* in 1966, changing his name after his father told him he would only become a screen star if he had an English name. He later joined the RSC but he made his name in the Oscar-winning film *Gandhi*. He has made a number of films, including *Schindler's List*, *Maurice* and *Fear is the Key*.

WWW.MANCHESTER2002-UK.COM

KWOUK, BERT (B. 1930)

Born in Manchester, Bert Kwouk grew up in Shanghai and returned to England in 1953. His first break was in the film *Inn of the Sixth Happiness*, but he made his name as the karate-mad servant in Peter Seller's *Pink Panther* films. He has had numerous other film and television roles, most notably in *Madam Sin*, *Goldfinger* and *You Only Live Twice*.

WWW.MANCHESTER2002-UK.COM

L

LANCASHIRE COUNTY CRICKET CLUB

Manchester Cricket Club was formed during the early 1800s and moved to Old Trafford in 1857. Lancashire County Cricket Club was formed in 1864 and became one of the most successful cricket clubs in the country. In 1884 Old Trafford 'became the second ground after The Oval to stage Test cricket' and 'with its stands, ladies tea room and pavilion, was regarded as second only to Lords'. On the day of the first Test match to be held there it poured with rain! Despite this, the second day attracted a crowd of 12,000 people.

The legendary Archie McClaren played his first game for Lancashire in 1890 while he was still a schoolboy, and scored a century against Sussex. He was one of LCC's greatest captains and in a match against Somerset scored 424 runs, a record which remained unbroken for ninety-nine years. In 1923, playing for England against New Zealand, he scored a double century and that record remains unbeaten.

There is a cricket Museum at Old Trafford which has a wide range of cricket memorabilia on display, including items belonging to W G Grace. The Museum is open on all 1st XI and international match days.

WWW.LCCC.CO.UK; FOR INFORMATION ABOUT THE MUSEUM CONTACT: KEITH HAYHURST, C/O LANCASHIRE CCC, OLD TRAFFORD, MANCHESTER M16 0PX.

LANCASTER HOUSE
Princess St. A large former textile warehouse stands at 80 Princess St next door to Asia House. Warehouse names tended to reflect trading areas. SIMON TAYLOR ET AL., *MANCHESTER: THE WAREHOUSE LEGACY* (2002).

LASS O' GOWRIE
Charles St. Pub close to the BBC with typical Victorian façade outside, wooden floors and comfort inside. An information board tells the story of Kitty who became 'Leddie Gowrie' to anyone who can read colloquial Scottish. The pub stands adjacent to the Charles St bridge over the River Medlock. Fixed to the wall overlooking the river is a plaque proudly marking the site of a urinal:

Sign on the side wall of the Lass o' Gowrie public house in Charles St.

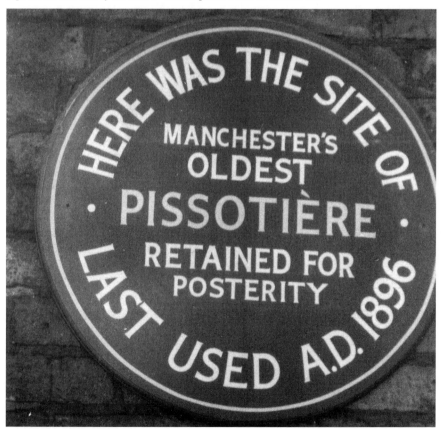

Here was the site of
Manchester's oldest
Pissotière
retained for
Posterity
Last used AD 1896

GLYNIS COOPER, *HIDDEN MANCHESTER* (2003).

LAW, DENIS (B. 1940)

A Scotsman by birth, Denis Law joined Manchester City FC in 1960. He was a 'midfield minder' with excellent goal-scoring abilities. After playing in seventy-seven matches and scoring thirty-seven goals, he briefly transferred to Torino in Italy before returning to join Manchester United FC where he played as a forward striker from 1962 to 1973. During his 393 appearances for United, Law scored 236 goals, including six against Luton during one match in 1961. He also won fifty-five Scottish caps.

WWW.MANCHESTER2002-UK.COM

LEVENSHULME

As late as 1844 Levenshulme (or Leofwine's island) was still 96 per cent meadowland and pasture. Gypsy caravans camped each year. The picturesquely wooded Nico Ditch, an unsuccessful earthen defence against the Danes, ran through the suburb. Slade Hall, a black and white timbered Tudor mansion, was built in 1585 by Edward and George Siddall. Stockport Rd (now the A6) was turnpiked in 1724 and half a century later the population had risen to the then huge number of 280. The toll bar stood on the corner of Slade Lane on the Longsight boundary because there was no road access to Levenshulme from other villages.

A cotton mill stood in Crowcroft Park, and there was a bleaching works in Pink Bank Lane; and there were also several light engineering works, a print works and Jackson's brick works in the suburb. For the most part, however, Levenshulme escaped the curse of the mills and, because of its semi-rural nature, had one of the lowest death rates in the country.

Today Levenshulme is home to many Asian families and the bright colours of their textiles, the temptingly spicy smells of their cooking and the richness of their culture have brought a cosmopolitan flavour to the area.

☛ *See also* SLADE HALL.

GLYNIS COOPER, *THE ILLUSTRATED HISTORY OF THE MANCHESTER SUBURBS* (2002); GAY SUSSEX ET AL., *LOOKING BACK AT LEVENSHULME AND BURNAGE* (1987).

LIBRARY THEATRE

St Peter's Square. The Library Theatre is so-called because it is situated in the basement of Central Library built in 1934 over the culverted River Tib. The theatre has a good reputation for the quality of dramatic production, ranging from Shakespeare to modern playwrights.

WWW.MANCHESTER2002-UK.COM

LINCOLN, ABRAHAM

Lincoln Square. Life-size model of the president on a large plinth on which are engraved extracts from letters sent by Lincoln to the cotton workers of Manchester during the American Civil War (1861–5). Although the war caused a cotton famine in Manchester, with mills shutting down or going on short time, which caused thousands of cotton mill workers severe hardship, the workers supported the fight against slavery wholeheartedly and sent messages of support to Abraham Lincoln. The statue commemorates their selfless action in showing solidarity with their fellow cotton workers. Ironically the black slave children of America enjoyed better hours and working conditions than English children who worked in the mills.

WWW.MANCHESTER2002-UK.COM

LIVERPOOL ROAD STATION

The oldest railway in Manchester was the Liverpool and Manchester Railway which opened on 15 September 1830. Liverpool Road Station marked its terminus. George Stephenson's *Rocket* locomotive was chosen to pull the passenger coaches. The station buildings and the warehouse built opposite in just five months during the 1830s are some of the oldest railway buildings in existence. The station was only in service between 1830 and 1844 and its buildings are now incorporated within the Museum of Science and Industry.

ALAN KIDD, *HISTORY OF MANCHESTER* (3RD EDN, 2002); WWW.MANCHESTER 2002-UK.COM

Sunday School built in 1911 on Liverpool Rd.

LONG MILLGATE

This used to run from the Cathedral along the banks of the Irk to where a corn mill and a fulling mill stood in earlier centuries; but is now truncated to a short lane along the side of Victoria Station and Chetham's College, mostly being subsumed by Corporation St and Dantzig St.
☛ *See also RISING SUN.*

Fountains in Cathedral Gardens lie along part of the former Long Millgate close to Poet's Corner (the Rising Sun), demolished 1923.

LONGSIGHT

Legend says that the name Longsight originated when one of Bonnie Prince Charlie's generals was heard to remark, on passing through the place, that 'it was a long sight to Manchester'. Grindlow Rd by the police station commemorates Grindlow Marsh which used to lie adjacent and it is possible that in former centuries Longsight was known as Grindlow. Longsight Hall used to stand opposite Grindlow Marsh.

The suburb grew up along the Stockport Rd (the present A6) next door to Levenshulme, and the boundaries are often blurred. There were no cotton mills but Longsight Silk Mill stood on Stockport Rd until it was destroyed by fire in 1869. In the 21st century Asian clothing manufacture is the main industry. Large railway maintenance/engineering workshops and engine sheds occupied a significant part of the northern sector of the suburb. Today they are used by Eurostar.

One of the most remarkable facts about Longsight is the amazing number and diversity of its churches. These included: St John's Church (built 1845–6) and the only church to have a graveyard; St Cyprian's Church which amalgamated with St John's in 1979; the Calvinist Methodist Church, known as the Welsh Church because it provided 'a spiritual home for Welsh exiles', which has now become Longsight Spiritualist Church; the College Chapel Methodist Church (1907–78) now the West Indian Church of the God of Prophecy; the First Church of Christ, Scientist (1903–78) mentioned by Nikolaus Pevsner in his books on English architecture; the Independent Chapel (known as the Ivy Chapel due to ivy growth on its walls); Longsight Free Christian Church (also known as the Unitarian Chapel) later used as a BBC van depot; the Tin Tabernacle (a Baptist church) now known as the Church of God, Seventh Day Adventists; the Ukrainian Orthodox Church; the Reformed Church of Jesus Christ and the Latter Day Saints; Roby Congregational Church (built 1911); the Methodist Church (1853–1966); Longsight Presbyterian Church (1870–1962); the Wesleyan Methodist Chapel; St Agnes Church (built 1885); St Clement's Church (built 1876, now demolished); St Robert's RC Church (built 1970).

☞ *See also* SLADE HALL.

GLYNIS COOPER, *THE ILLUSTRATED HISTORY OF THE MANCHESTER SUBURBS* (2002); GAY SUSSEX, *LONGSIGHT PAST AND PRESENT* (1982).

LOST CANAL

In 1787 the Duke of Bridgewater built another canal to run partly through an underground tunnel beneath the city which would carry coals from Castlefield to the coal wharf at Bank Top (now Piccadilly Railway Station). This canal is very badly silted up and barely visible except as an almost submerged entrance from the Medlock on the south side of Asia House.

G. ASHWORTH, *THE LOST RIVERS OF MANCHESTER* (1987).

LOVELL, SIR BERNARD (B. 1913)

Sir Bernard Lovell was Professor of Radio Astronomy at Manchester University and Director of Jodrell Bank Radio Telescope from 1951 to 1980. The world's first radar transmitter and receiver were installed by Lovell at Jodrell Bank, Cheshire, in December 1945. The telescope was operational from August 1957. It tracked the world's first artificial satellite and has been involved in many astronomy and space research projects. Today the observatory has eight telescopes and work on the behaviour of meteors has gradually shifted to cosmic radio waves emanating from deep space.
WWW.MANCHESTER2002-UK.COM

LOWRY, L S (1887–1976)

Lawrence Stephen Lowry was the only child of Irish parents and was born in Rusholme. He was educated at a school in Victoria Park and then attended Manchester College of Art and Salford School of Art. Lowry lived in Salford for forty years, becoming renowned for his paintings of the Salford and Manchester millscapes peopled by small stick-like figures who were immortalized in the popular song 'Matchstick Men ... and Matchstick Cats and Dogs'. In 1945 he was awarded an honorary MA by Manchester University and he became a member of the Royal Academy in 1962. He finally settled in Mottram on the edge of the wild and beautiful Longdendale Valley linking Manchester to West Yorkshire. Here he continued to paint millscapes which he could not see (the mills had disappeared from the valley by this time) but which he could still feel. He died in 1976 and a Blue Plaque marks the house where he spent his final years.
WWW.MANCHESTER2002-UK.COM

LOWRY, SUNNY (B. 1911)

Born in Longsight and educated at the Manchester High School for Girls, Sunny Lowry became the first woman to swim the English Channel. She began swimming at the Victoria Baths and then trained with her sister for competitions at Levenshulme Baths. She was successful at her third attempt to swim the Channel on 28 August 1933 when she swam from Cap Gris Nez to St Margarets (near Folkstone) in 15 hours 41 minutes.
WWW.MANCHESTER2002-UK.COM

LOWRY, THE

The Lowry is part of the docks regeneration scheme and is built on the site of the former No. 9 Dock. The project takes its name from one of Salford's most famous sons, the internationally renowned painter L S Lowry. The Lowry complex includes the Lyric Theatre and the Quays Theatre; art galleries which display the work of L S Lowry; bars, cafes, shops, information centres and Artworks (a creative community project); the Digital World Centre; a unique lifting footbridge over the Ship Canal; and the Imperial War Museum.

☞ *See also L S LOWRY; IMPERIAL WAR MUSEUM NORTH.*
WWW.THELOWRY.COM

LYALL, GRAHAM THOMPSON (1892-1941)
He was born in Manchester but emigrated to Canada. However, Graham Lyall returned to England in September 1915 and was sent to France where he served until June 1916 with the 4th Canadian Mounted Rifles. In 1918 he was awarded the Victoria Cross for 'conspicuous bravery and skilful leadership north of Cambrai'. He was promoted to major and served as an Ordnance mechanical engineer. He was killed on active service in the Western Desert during the Second World War.
WWW.MANCHESTER2002-UK.COM

M

MCCONNELL AND KENNEDY
Cotton spinning machine makers who later turned to cotton spinning based in Ancoats from the end of the 18th century. Kennedy withdrew from the partnership during the early 19th century but McConnell's went on to become a very successful cotton manufacturing enterprise. Towards the end of the 19th century they amalgamated with Murray Brothers of Ancoats to become Manchester Fine Spinners.
WWW.SPINNINGTHEWEB.ORG.UK

MACINTOSH, CHARLES (1766–1843)
Charles Macintosh was a Scottish chemist who discovered how to produce dissolved India rubber from coal gas and by joining two sheets of fabric together with this new rubber solution, he invented a new material that was waterproof. Macintosh went into business with Thomas Hancock and developed a manufacturing process for the production of waterproofed sheets and coats. His new rainproof coat became known as a 'Mackintosh'. In 1840 he moved to Hulme in Manchester where he established a factory on Cambridge St producing waterproof clothing. In the early 20th century the famous name of Dunlop took over the works.
GLYNIS COOPER, *ILLUSTRATED HISTORY OF THE MANCHESTER SUBURBS* (2002); WWW.MANCHESTER2002-UK.COM

MANCHESTER AIRPORT
☞ *See WYTHENSHAWE.*

MANCHESTER AIRPORT CRASHES

The first fatal plane crash was in 1951 when a Dakota crashed, killing its crew of two. The first passenger disaster occurred in 1957 when a Viscount crashed killing a total of 22 people. Possibly the most celebrated crash happened on 22 August 1985 when a Boeing 737 carrying 131 passengers and six crew on a flight to Corfu crashed after an explosion in one of the engines ignited a fuel tank. Though the captain aborted take-off he turned the aircraft into the wind which blew the fire onto the rear fuselage. Most of the 54 people died as a result of inhaling toxic gases. Two of the air hostesses died trying to help passengers to safety; a third survived by crawling on her hands and knees down the aisle to help passengers thereby avoiding the worst effects of the toxic fumes. All three were awarded the Queen's Gallantry Medal.

WWW.MANCHESTER2002-UK.COM

MANCHESTER AND SALFORD EQUITABLE CO-OPERATIVE SOCIETY, THE CWS

The original Co-operative Society was formed in Rochdale so that workers could buy goods wholesale and therefore more cheaply. The idea caught on quickly and by 1880 Manchester CWS had nineteen branches, with its headquarters in Ardwick. The CWS worked on a multiple stores basis and included drapery, tailoring, boots, shoes, butchery and grocery departments. A 'dividend' was offered as a 'loyalty payment' to customers who shopped with the CWS.

WWW.MANCHESTER2002-UK.COM

MANCHESTER AND SALFORD JUNCTION CANAL

An underground canal which ran north from the Rochdale Canal to the River Irwell, from where boats could navigate to Bolton, Bury and Warrington. It was built in 1839 and was less than a mile in length although it had four locks. It passes beneath the Great Northern Railway Warehouse on Watson St and Granada Television Studios in Quay St. The canal closed in 1922 and was partly infilled but some of the tunnel was used as an air raid shelter during the Second World War.

ALAN KIDD, *HISTORY OF MANCHESTER* (3RD EDN, 2002).

MANCHESTER AQUATICS CENTRE

A purpose-built swimming pool complex, costing £30 million, located in the University campus on Oxford Rd, about half a mile south of the city centre. Completed in October 2000, the Aquatics Centre offers two Olympic-standard pools where swimming, diving and synchronized swimming events can take place; and including seating facilities for 2,500 people. There is also an additional 50m pool for athlete training.

WWW.MANCHESTER2002-UK.COM

MANCHESTER CITY FOOTBALL CLUB

Manchester City grew out of St Mark's Football Club formed in West Gorton in 1880. Their first playing field was a piece of waste ground at Clowes St. The Club underwent several name changes, including Gorton Football Club and Ardwick Football Club, finally adopting Manchester City in 1894. The team reached the Football League's Second Division in 1892 and the First Division in 1899. Their Welsh winger Billy Meredith scored twenty-nine League goals but he moved to Manchester United in 1903. City's Hyde Rd ground was destroyed by fire in 1920 and the Club moved to a purpose-built ground at Maine Rd on the edge of Moss Side in 1923. After the Commonwealth Games of 2002 were over Manchester City adopted the new Sportcity Stadium as their permanent home. Known locally as 'the Blues', there is great rivalry between City and United, 'the Reds'.

WWW.MCFC.CO.UK

MANCHESTER COTTONS

These were not cottons but a fine napped woollen weave produced by the descendants of the 14th-century Flemish weavers who had settled in Manchester and who were skilled in weaving flax, wool and silk. In 1552 an Act was passed to control the quality of Manchester Cottons.

WWW.SPINNINGTHEWEB.ORG.UK

MANCHESTER EYE HOSPITAL

Oxford Rd. Established in 1814 and now part of a complex which includes the nearby medical school and Manchester Royal Infirmary.

WWW.CMHT.NWEST.NHS.UK/HOSPITALS

MANCHESTER FOOD RIOTS

During the latter part of the 18th century food and corn prices rose at a pace totally out of step with wages. In desperation and hunger Manchester citizens begged for fair prices for food. When their pleas fell on deaf ears they took the law into their own hands. In 1757 there were food riots on Shude Hill and a wall plaque commemorates four deaths and fifteen injured as a result during the night of 14/15 November.

There were a number of food riots during the 1790s for the same reasons. One of the worst took place on 30 July 1795 in the Market Place. The crowd was dispersed by a cavalry charge and several people were injured. The last food riots in Manchester were in 1812, although the Corn Laws (which kept the price of grain artificially high) were not repealed until the 1830s.

GLYNIS COOPER, *HIDDEN MANCHESTER* (2004).

MANCHESTER GRAMMAR SCHOOL

Old Hall Lane. Prestigious boys-only grammar school founded in 1515 by Hugh Oldham. The school has moved premises several times and at one time occupied Chetham's College. During the 1930s, the present school was built on the former Birch Hall estate. In 1874 Manchester Girls High School was built in nearby Rusholme 'to provide for Manchester's daughters what has been provided without stint for Manchester's sons'.

WWW.MGS.ORG.UK

MANCHESTER MARTYRS (1867)

These were three Irish Fenians named William O'Mera Allen, Michael Larkin and William O'Brien. The Fenians were an Irish-American secret society, who were anti-British. They were founded in 1858 to campaign for support of armed rebellion after the death of the Irish nationalist leader, Daniel O'Connell. On 11 September 1867 Fenian Colonel Thomas Kelly and Captain Timothy Deasy were arrested in Manchester. A week later, as they were being taken from the Manchester Courts to the gaol on Hyde Rd in West Gorton (Strangeways did not open until 1868), the closed van in which they were locked and handcuffed was ambushed underneath a railway arch. Twelve mounted police were escorting the prisoners but about thirty men took part in the ambush, grabbing the horses and overpowering the escort. The police sergeant inside the van with the prisoners, Sergeant Brett, refused to open the door so attempts were made to force it. The sergeant put his eye to the keyhole to see what was happening as one of the ambushers fired a pistol through the keyhole in frustration. The bullet hit Sergeant Brett in the eye and passed through to his brain, killing him instantly. Eventually the door was forced open. Colonel Kelly and Captain Deasy escaped into history and were never recaptured. The ambushers then ran for their lives but the police gave chase and managed to arrest five men: William O'Mera Allen, Michael Larkin, William O'Brien, Thomas Maguire and Edward Stone. They were tried and four were found guilty and sentenced to death. Thomas Maguire was pardoned and discharged. Edward Stone's sentence was commuted to life imprisonment (in the 19th century life imprisonment meant just that; not fifteen years reduced to ten for good behaviour); but the remaining three were hanged on 23 November 1867. A memorial was later erected to them in Moston cemetery and there is a commemorative plaque to Sergeant Brett in St Ann's Church on St Ann's Square.

WWW.MANCHESTER2002-UK.COM

MANCHESTER MUMMY

Miss Hannah Beswick of Birchin Bower died in 1785 at Cheetwood Hall in Manchester. She had an absolute horror of being buried alive and so she left her doctor a sum of money on the condition that she was never buried below ground. Her body was embalmed by Dr White, a founder of Manchester Royal Infirmary, and initially she was kept at Ancoats Hall where a member of the Beswick family lived. Perhaps the family found this a bit gruesome because she was removed to a specially constructed room at the top of The Priory in Sale, the residence of Dr White. After his death she was placed in the care of Dr Ollier, and was subsequently given to the Manchester Museum in Peter St where she became known as the 'Manchester Mummy'. When the Manchester Museum was transferred to Manchester University a meeting of the trustees and medical representatives was held to decide what to do with the 'Mummy of Birchin Bower'. They took into account her wishes and her pathological fear of being buried alive, but finally decided that, after 83 years, she was 'irrevocably and unmistakeably dead'. Consequently she was buried in the Harpurhey Cemetery on 12 July 1868.
WWW.MYSTERIOUSBRITAIN.CO.UK

MANCHESTER METROPOLITAN UNIVERSITY

All Saints, Oxford Rd. MMU, as it is known locally, was formerly Manchester Polytechnic and gained university status in 1992. The Polytechnic was founded in 1970 as an amalgam of Manchester College of Art and Design, Manchester College of Commerce, John Dalton College of Technology, to which were added in 1977 Didsbury College of Education and Hollings College (the Domestic and Trades College whose 'toast rack' building was opened in 1960 on Wilmslow Rd), followed by the City of Manchester College of Higher Education in 1983. Around 1993 Crewe and Alsager College of Higher Education also became part of MMU.
WWW.MMU.AC.UK

MANCHESTER MUSEUM

Oxford Rd. The present museum collection of six million items was begun with collections by Manchester Society of Natural History and the Manchester Geological and Mining Society. In 1867 Owens College (now part of the University of Manchester) took responsibility for the collections and commissioned Alfred Waterhouse (who designed Manchester Town Hall) to design a museum. Manchester Museum first opened in 1885. In 1912 a 'Pavilion' was added to accommodate archaeological collections, followed by an extension in 1927 for the ethnographic collections.

Today the museum houses collections on animals, archaeology, archery, coins, Egyptology, fossils, living animals, living cultures, plants, rocks and

minerals. Galleries are devoted to subjects such as prehistoric life, archaeology, dinosaurs and science for life.
HTTP://MUSEUM.MAN.AC.UK

MANCHESTER REFORM CLUB
This three-storey building, designed by Edward Solomons and built by John Philpot-Jones in 1870–1 on King St, was one of the last to be built in the popular Venetian Gothic style of the time. It had a parapet with a balustrade, gable end towers, spires and balconies beneath windows on the lower floors. A wood-panelled staircase led up to the billiard room. In keeping with Victorian ostentatiousness, marble-lined lavatories were installed in the 1890s in the belief that these were quite fitting for the place in which the city's gentry took their relaxation.
WWW.MANCHESTER2002-UK.COM

MANCHESTER ROYAL INFIRMARY
Formerly stood on the site of Piccadilly Plaza. The sunken gardens with the fountains used to be the hospital's lake. The hospital moved in 1902 to Stanley Grove off Oxford Rd and is now Manchester's major hospital.
WWW.CMHT.NWEST.NHS.UK/HOSPITALS

Manchester New Royal Infirmary, 1909, which stands on Oxford Rd.

MANCHESTER SHIP CANAL

The Ship Canal was built to link Manchester with the sea so that the city could trade internationally without incurring the prohibitive port charges levied by Liverpool and the high cost of transporting freight by railway. Construction of the Ship Canal was begun in 1887 and completed in 1894. It was a massive undertaking. Plant used included 75 steam excavators, 124 steam cranes, and 7 earth dredgers. The depth to which the Canal was dug was the same as the Suez Canal. It was 35 miles long with triple entrance locks. James Brindley achieved a unique feat of engineering by building the Barton Aqueduct which carried the Bridgewater Canal over the Ship Canal.

A triumphal arch was built to accompany the opening of the Manchester Ship Canal by Queen Victoria in 1894. The docks for the canal lay in three main units: Trafford Rd, Trafford Wharf and the shallower Pomona Docks built on the former site of the Pomona Pleasure Gardens. Trafford Park Industrial Estate, the world's first industrial estate, developed adjacent to the canal. By 1914 the Manchester and Salford Docks had captured 5 per cent of the UK import market and 4.4 per cent of the domestic exports market. ALAN KIDD, *HISTORY OF MANCHESTER* (3RD EDN, 2002).

MANCHESTER UNITED FOOTBALL CLUB

Manchester United originated as the football team of Newton Heath Traction Maintenance Depot whose logo was a witch in a pointed hat riding her broomstick. The football team of the company was initially known as The Heathens, partly because of the name Heath and partly because of the witch logo. The Heathens became a professional football team in 1885 and changed their name to Manchester United in 1902. In 1886 they won their first trophy, the Manchester Senior Cup. By 1902, however, the team were in financial difficulties. Full-back Harry Stafford led efforts to raise funds, as a result of which John Davies, a local brewery owner, bought the club and it was he who introduced the red and white stripes. In 1903 United employed their first manager, Ernest Magnell, a very fit man who drove his team hard and bought talented players, including Billy Meredith who was the Beckham of his day and led his team to their first League title, which established United's reputation for quality football. It is a tradition which the current manager, Sir Alex Ferguson, has sought to maintain. A year later Manchester United won the FA Cup against Bristol City. The club moved to Old Trafford in 1910.
☛ *See also MUNICH AIR DISASTER.*
WWW.MANUTD.COM

MANNING, BERNARD (B. 1930)

A comedian born in the millscapes of Ancoats, he grew up in Blackley and later bought an old billiard hall which he turned into the Embassy Club in

Harpurhey. Mike Yarwood, Matt Monroe and Jimmy Tarbuck all performed at the club. Bernard Manning himself found fame through *The Comedians* on Granada Television.
WWW.MANCHESTER2002-UK.COM

MARKET PLACE

The original market place and trading centre of Manchester was situated, according to Green's map of 1787, on the site of the present Exchange Square and the new Marks and Spencer. The market cross, the hub around which the life of the market revolved, would, as shown on Green's map, have stood approximately in the middle of the Per Una and designer fashion departments of Marks and Spencer. In earlier centuries the town beadle announced the opening of the market each Saturday from the steps of the market cross by ringing his bell. Near the cross stood the pillory, the stocks and the public whipping post. The beadle would announce the offences of various miscreants from the cross before punishments were meted out: 'rogues and vagabonds were whipped; drunks were placed in the stocks; fraudulent traders in the pillory'.

Market St, c.1922.

Bread, meat, poultry, eggs, cheese, fish, vegetables, ale, spices, cloth, saddles, etc. were sold in the market. The conduit, which supplied fresh water to the townspeople, also stood in the market place near the pillory. People came to trade, to shop, to gossip. The market place was the centre of the town's commercial and social life. Today shopping centres and supermarkets have taken over; although the subterranean food department of Marks and Spencer with its central coffee shop still reflects the original purpose of the old market on its former site. There is no longer a separate market place in Manchester but Market St, with its shops, indoor market and the Arndale Centre, carries forward something of the old market tradition.
'THE OLD MARKET CROSS AT MANCHESTER', *LANCASHIRE STORIES* (*C.*1905), PP. 443–6.

MARKS AND SPENCER – BUSINESS

In 1884 a Russian Jewish refugee, Michael Marks, opened a penny bazaar stall in Leeds. He moved to 20 Cheetham Hill Rd in 1893 and opened a penny bazaar there. Legend says his slogan was 'don't ask the price, it's a penny' because his command of English was poor. In 1894 he went into partnership with Tom Spencer and the world-famous company of Marks and Spencer was born. They opened their first warehouse and head office on Derby St in 1901. Their trademark was quality clothing at affordable prices. Marks and Spencer became a public company in 1926; and in 1931 food departments were introduced to some of the stores. In recent years however it was feared that Marks and Spencer were losing touch with changing tastes and there have been a number of new fashion initiatives for the 21st century.
WWW.FAIRCOMMENT.COM

MARKS AND SPENCER – SHOP

Marks and Spencer's store was completely destroyed by the 1996 IRA bomb. The new store stands on the site of the former market place and is the largest Marks and Spencer store in the world. It sells clothing, soft furnishings, toiletries, food, and small gifts and there is a coffee shop in the basement.
☛ *See also* CHEETHAM.
WWW.MANCHESTER2002-UK.COM

MATHER AND PLATT

In 1845 the Mather family and John Platt of Salford Iron Works went into partnership to produce and service textile finishing machines. Sir William Mather (1838–1920) became head of the Mather and Platt Salford Iron Works Engineering Company. He was described as 'an industrialist, entrepreneur, humanitarian and politician who put the welfare of his workers of equal importance alongside profit'. In 1883 he purchased the patent to the

Grinnell Sprinkler System for the whole world except America, as a result of which Mather and Platt became leaders in the British sprinkler industry. He introduced an eight hour working day at the Iron Works in 1893.
WWW.MANCHESTER2002-UK.COM

MECHANICS INSTITUTE, PRINCESS STREET
☛ *See PEOPLE'S HISTORY MUSEUM.*

MEDIEVAL MANCHESTER
The barony of Manchester was made up of the 'demesne manors' of Manchester and Withington, which included all the present-day suburbs (except Northenden and what is now Wythenshawe), and Salford Manor, Barton-on-Irwell Manor, Ashton Manor; Heaton Norris Manor, and land around Horwich, which make up much of the modern area of Greater Manchester.

The manor house stood on the site now occupied by Chetham's College. There was a mill for grinding corn on Long Millgate and a fulling mill by the River Irk. A survey of 1282 records two water-driven corn mills on the banks of the Irk. The Court Baron (a sort of superior magistrate's court) met every three weeks. The lord could 'claim liberty of the gallows, the pit, the pillory and the tumbril'. A market was held each Saturday and, after 1227, there was an annual fair held each September.

In 1301, Thomas Grelly, the last of the Grelly line, granted the inhabitants a charter whose thirty-four clauses would regulate local government until 1846. The barony passed into the hands of the de la Warre family in 1309. Thomas de la Warre obtained collegiate college status for the parish church of St Mary's and rebuilt the manor house as a small college. During the 1330s a number of Flemish immigrants settled in the area, bringing their weaving skills with them which they passed on to local people.
GLYNIS COOPER, *ILLUSTRATED HISTORY OF THE MANCHESTER SUBURBS* (2002).

MEN VICTORIA STATION
Hunts Bank. The Manchester Evening News Arena was built in 1995 as 'the biggest multipurpose indoor entertainment/sports arena in Europe'. It is home to the Manchester Storm Ice Hockey Team and the Manchester Giants Basketball Team. Storm and Giants games usually take place on Saturdays and Sundays in winter. Netball and boxing competitions are also staged here. The arena can seat between 7,000 and 21,000 people and hosts major musical events of both classical and popular genres. The Nynex, built on the site of the former Exchange Station which adjoined Victoria Station, can seat 19,500 people and has hosted performances by internationally renowned artists such as the Three Tenors (Placido Domingo, José Careras

and Luciano Pavarotti), Celine Dion, Simply Red, Barry Manilow and Eric Clapton.
WWW.MANCHESTER2002-UK.COM

MERCHANTS WAREHOUSE

Castlefield. The Merchants Warehouse was built off Catalan Square in 1825. Like the Middle Warehouse it had twin or paired 'shipping holes' to internal docks and external goods doors with hoists. It was damaged by fire in 1971 but the building survived and in 1976 it was converted into luxury offices and apartments. Weeping willow trees have now been planted around as part of a landscaping exercise.
GLYNIS COOPER, *HIDDEN MANCHESTER* (2004); SIMON TAYLOR ET AL., *MANCHESTER: THE WAREHOUSE LEGACY* (2002).

Merchants Warehouse at Castlefield showing 'twin shipping holes' to internal docks. Building now houses apartments and offices.

Market St, Manchester, c.1907: the trams are following roughly the present-day Metrolink lines.

METROLINK

The tram-train system of the Metrolink currently has three lines: to Bury, to Altrincham and to Eccles and Salford Quays; although new lines to Ashton and to the airport have been considered. The first line to open was the Bury-Manchester line in the mid-1990s. The wheel appears to have come full circle

Metrolink soars over the canal basin at Castlefield.

since the closure of local railway lines and the withdrawal of road tram services during the middle decades of the 20th century.
ALAN KIDD, *HISTORY OF MANCHESTER* (3RD EDN, 2002); WWW.MANCHESTER 2002-UK.COM

MIDDLE WAREHOUSE
Castlefield. Middle Warehouse was built in 1828–31 at the head of the Middle Basin. It had twin 'shipping holes' to internal docks and external goods doors with hoists. Today there is a wooden bridge across the canal basin to allow easy pedestrian access. Most of the warehouse has been transformed into luxury apartments but on the ground floor there is now an upmarket restaurant named Choice. The parquet flooring, gleaming glass and silverware and the elegant menu are in sharp contrast with the original industrial use and basic facilities of the building.
GLYNIS COOPER, *HIDDEN MANCHESTER* (2004); SIMON TAYLOR ET AL., *MANCHESTER: THE WAREHOUSE LEGACY* (2002).

MILES PLATTING
The suburb is said to take its name from the place where plaited rushes were laid across a stream to ford it about a mile from the city centre. Miles Platting is one of the smaller and newer suburbs, a child of the Industrial Revolution. It was home to Victoria Mills, Holland's Mill, Ducie Mills; to Morgan and Crossleys, Hardman and Holdens; the Providence Works, a chemical works, a timber yard, a forge, a tannery, and a gas works which stood on Bradford Rd together with ten public houses.

Currently Miles Platting is part of the East Manchester Regeneration Scheme. There is the Carrioca Business Park (near the quaintly named Spanking Roger public house named after Roger Aytoun, a Scottish soldier who married a local heiress) and the Victoria Mills have been converted and refurbished as a community centre and city centre living quarters. The apartments on the upper four floors are luxurious with parquet flooring and all mod cons but something of the millscapes still lingers and they do not have a homely air about them.
GLYNIS COOPER, *THE ILLUSTRATED HISTORY OF THE MANCHESTER SUBURBS* (2002); FRED ROBERTS, *MEMORIES OF A VICTORIAN CHILDHOOD AND WORKING LIFE IN MILES PLATTING* (1986).

MODAHL, DIANE (B. 1966)
Manchester born and bred Diane Modahl has won the 800m Commonwealth medal three times and she won a gold medal in Auckland in 1990 when she broke the 800m record. So far she has won the British 800m six times and she has taken part in four Olympic Games. In 1994 she faced

drugs charges and was sent home from the Commonwealth Games in disgrace. It took two years to clear her name but finally the International Amateur Athletics Federation admitted the tests had been flawed and the British Athletic Federation reinstated her professional status. During this time she gained a BA in media and business management at Manchester University. In the 1998 Commonwealth Games she won a bronze medal for the 800m. Subsequently she played a major part in the television reporting of the 2002 Commonwealth Games in her home city. She now works in sports journalism and as a sports presenter on BBC Greater Manchester Radio. WWW.MANCHESTER2002-UK.COM

MOORS MURDERS

Ian Brady (b. 1938) and Myra Hindley (1942-2002) became known as the Moors Murderers in the mid-1960s. Myra Hindley was born and brought up in Gorton. She was a religious girl who led a fairly dull life and she wanted excitement. Glasgow-born Ian Brady was dark and good-looking and he had served time in Strangeways. Myra fell head over heels in love with him and from that moment on she was lost. Pauline Reade was a girl of Myra's acquaintance and Myra sometimes babysat for the Reade family. On that fateful July day in 1963 16-year-old Pauline had no reason to be afraid when she got into the car with Myra Hindley and Ian Brady. A few hours later she was dead; sexually assaulted and murdered by the couple who buried her body on the lonely windswept Saddleworth Moor. In October that year they gave a lift to a 12-year-old lad from Ashton-under-Lyne named John Kilbride. He was never seen alive again. The following year 10-year-old Lesley Ann Downey was abducted, assaulted and strangled at their home in Hattersley near Glossop. This time Brady taped the murder. When the tape was played at their trial, the cries of pain, fear and the pleas for her life made by little Lesley Ann reduced the court to tears. Next to die was 12-year-old Keith Bennett and his body was also buried on Saddleworth Moor, but despite intensive police searches it has never been found. In 1965 17-year-old Edward Evans was tortured before being killed. This time however there had been a witness: Hindley's brother-in-law, David Smith. Sickened, he called the police and put an end to Brady and Hindley's reign of torture, terror and murder. The case became known as the Moors Murders because of their habit of burying their victims on Saddleworth Moor. Myra Hindley conducted a campaign for parole from the mid-1980s onward but though she appeared remorseful for her crimes she seemed to understand neither how dreadful the acts in which she had participated were and the public revulsion against her, nor the pain she was causing her victim's families. She was taken ill and died in West Suffolk General Hospital before the matter of her parole was resolved. Ian Brady has expressed no desire for release and accepts that

he will die in prison. The more intelligent of the pair, he at least understands what would await him outside the walls.
GLYNIS COOPER, THE ILLUSTRATED HISTORY OF THE MANCHESTER SUBURBS (2002); WWW.MANCHESTER2002-UK.COM

MOSLEY STREET

Mosley St/Lower Mosley St takes its name from the Mosley family who owned several estates in the Manchester area, and runs from Piccadilly to the GMEX (formerly Central Station). The elegant Georgian merchants' houses were replaced in 19th century with warehouses, some of which survive, including Richard Cobden's 'palazzo-style' warehouse at nos. 14–18. The Portico Library also fronts onto Mosley St.
☛ See also COBDEN'S WAREHOUSE.

MOSS SIDE

At the beginning of the 19th century Moss Side was a picturesque hamlet of small farms and a population of just 150 people on the edge of a moss, where Victorian ladies had their picnics in rich green meadows full of buttercups. In 1848 Elizabeth Gaskell featured Pepperhill Farm (demolished in 1900) in her novel *Mary Barton* and describes the idyllic rural scenes of Moss Side. The last farm in Moss Side was still a working farm in 1900.

The roads are laid out in a grid system due to modern planning rather than natural evolution. Workers' houses built here were of better quality owing to their mostly being built after the new building regulations of the mid-19th century. Parts of Moss Side were regarded as quite genteel, especially the area around Alexandra Park (opened 1876) and Greenheys around Denmark Rd. Sir Charles Hallé, who gave his name to the Hallé Orchestra, lived here and Rupert Potter, father of the writer Beatrix Potter, was born at 208 Exmouth Rd in 1833. Friedrich Engels rented 63–65 Cecil St during the 1840s and sometimes Karl Marx stayed here as his guest.

In the 1960s Moss Side boasted a yam-yam shop which sold West Indian produce, a testament to the growing multicultural nature of the suburb; and until recently Maine Rd was home to the 'Blues' of Manchester City Football Club.
GLYNIS COOPER, THE ILLUSTRATED HISTORY OF THE MANCHESTER SUBURBS (2002);
CHRIS MAKEPEACE, LOOKING BACK AT HULME, MOSS SIDE, CHORLTON-ON-MEDLOCK AND ARDWICK (1998).

MOSS SIDE AND HULME PARTNERSHIP 1997

Regeneration scheme which instigated the rebuilding of housing in Hulme and Moss Side involving local communities; the improvement of Princess Rd;

the renovation of the Alexandra Park housing estate; the establishment of Birley Fields Business Park; and the development of Hulme High St.
ALAN KIDD, *HISTORY OF MANCHESTER* (3RD EDN, 2002); WWW.MANCHESTER 2002-UK.COM

MOSTON

Moston was originally a farmstead on the marshes but it had grown into a village by 1100. Parts were still rural in 1911. There were thatched cottages in Moston until the 20th century and the intriguingly named Coffin Well in Moston Bottoms. Over the centuries five halls were built: Moston Hall, Great Nuthurst Hall, Little Nuthurst Hall, Lightbowne Hall and Hough Hall. By 1900 the first three were in ruins and Lightbowne Hall was demolished in 1965.

Bowking, the washing and bleaching of linen, was a cottage industry in Moston from Tudor times until the 19th century when bleaching and dye works sprang up along the Dean Brook. In addition there were silk handloom weavers and one of them, William Simpson, endowed the Simpson Memorial Institute which houses the public library today. Moston also had a colliery which had four shafts, all abandoned in turn; the last in 1950. Moston Village remains very pleasant and it is home to the Drawing Room Restaurant, a name evocative of a bygone age.
GLYNIS COOPER, *THE ILLUSTRATED HISTORY OF THE MANCHESTER SUBURBS* (2002); BRIAN SEARLE, *MOSTON STORY* (1983).

MOSTON COLLIERY

Moston had a colliery which was operative from 1840 to 1950. The first shaft was sunk in 1840; the second in 1850. Both of these were abandoned in 1886. A third shaft had been sunk in 1884, the deepest one, and the fourth and final one, the shallowest, was sunk close by in 1887. On the morning of 11 March 1940 seven trucks derailed and crashed to the bottom of No. 17 slant. Six miners were killed and fifteen were injured. The colliery closed ten years afterwards and an estate for workers from Bradford Colliery in Central Manchester was built on the site.
GLYNIS COOPER, *THE ILLUSTRATED HISTORY OF THE MANCHESTER SUBURBS* (2002).

MR THOMAS'S CHOP HOUSE

Cross St. The Chop House, a narrow three-storey town house, was opened as a pub and restaurant in 1867 by Thomas Studd whose Christian name gave the place its name. Chop houses date back to Stuart times when business dinners consisted simply of plates of cooked or grilled meat and large quantities of ale or wine. To step through the door is to step back in

time. The decor, menu and serving staff are straight from Edwardian England. It is also a Real Ale pub. There is no canned music, no flashy lighting, no fake beams and no fast food in sight. Charles Dickens would have felt quite at home here. It is a great place to try traditional old northern dishes like black pudding, hotpot, steak and kidney pudding, potato cakes, bacon and cabbage.
GLYNIS COOPER, *HIDDEN MANCHESTER* (2003).

MUNICH AIR DISASTER
The Munich Air Disaster and the Busby Babes are enshrined in United history and engraved on the hearts of older fans. In February 1958 a plane carrying the Manchester United team, known as the Busby Babes, crashed in snow on take-off at Munich Airport. They were returning from a match against Red Star Belgrade which they had drawn 3–3, winning themselves a place in the European Cup semi-finals. Seven players, eight journalists and three club officials were killed. An eighth player died later from his injuries. Matt Busby, the manager, Bobby Charlton and defender Bill Foulkes survived. United were shattered but fought back. It took ten years for Matt Busby to replace his original Babes with a winning team, but he finally succeeded and in 1968 the new team stormed to victory in the European Cup with a 4–1 win against Benfica at Wembley Stadium. The 'Munich Clock' above the entrance to Old Trafford is a permanent remembrance of those who died in 1958 and displays the hour and date of the disaster, its hands stopped forever as a mark of respect at the exact time the plane crashed.
☛ *See also MANCHESTER UNITED FOOTBALL CLUB.*
WWW.MANUTD.COM

MURRAY BROTHERS
George and Adam Murray were cotton spinning machine makers who later turned to cotton spinning based in Ancoats from the end of the 18th century. They built some of the earliest mills in Ancoats. Towards the end of the 19th century they amalgamated with McConnells to become Manchester Fine Spinners.
WWW.SPINNINGTHEWEB.ORG.UK

MURRAY MILL
Ancoats. An early steam-driven mill, built in 1798 by the Murray Brothers, Adam and George, who were initially spinning machine makers before using their own machines to become cotton spinners.
ROBINA MCNEIL AND MICHAEL NEVELL, *A GUIDE TO THE INDUSTRIAL ARCHAEOLOGY OF GREATER MANCHESTER* (2000); MIKE WILLIAMS WITH D A FARNIE, *COTTON MILLS IN GREATER MANCHESTER* (1992).

MURRAY MILLS COMPLEX

Ancoats. The fourth side of the courtyard made by Murray Mill, Decker Mill and Jersey Street New Mill infilled with smaller buildings. The courtyard is entered by a 'Great Gate' and within it a canal basin was built and linked by a tunnel to the Rochdale Canal.

ROBINA MCNEIL AND MICHAEL NEVELL, *A GUIDE TO THE INDUSTRIAL ARCHAEOLOGY OF GREATER MANCHESTER* (2000); MIKE WILLIAMS WITH D A FARNIE, *COTTON MILLS IN GREATER MANCHESTER* (1992).

MUSEUM OF LABOUR HISTORY, BRIDGE STREET

This museum, based in an Edwardian pumping station, is dedicated to working-class history and includes the Suffragette Movement, over 300 banners of trade unions and workers groups, Peterloo, the Co-operative Society, work and life in the millscapes. Much more archive material is held in the former TUC building on Princess St and there are also textile conservation facilities. The Trades Union Congress took place there in June 1868. Many early members received beautifully inscribed certificates of their trade union membership.
WWW.MANCHESTER2002-UK.COM

Rear of the Edwardian pump house which houses the Museum of Labour History.

MUSEUM OF SCIENCE AND INDUSTRY

Liverpool Rd. The museum is based around the former Liverpool Road Railway Station which was only in service 1830–1844. Behind one of the old platforms is an 1830s warehouse erected in just five months by Manchester builder David Bellhouse. This is a listed building, as is the main building which is a Great Western Railway warehouse of the 1880s. There has been little change to

Museum of Science and Industry on Liverpool Rd.

this warehouse, which includes a Victorian office, a hydraulic crane and gas lighting. There is also a 'Power Hall' and an 'Air and Space Hall'.

There are a number of galleries and displays featuring themes and artefacts from the science and technology of the 18th- and 19th-century Industrial Revolution as well as some of the early computers from the 20th century. The museum also holds a large textile archive including pattern books and the notebooks of William Perkin who discovered the first synthetic dyes in 1858, as well as the records of Manchester scientists such as John Dalton, James Joule, Bernard Lovell and Ernest Rutherford.

☛ *See also* JOHN DALTON; JAMES JOULE; BERNARD LOVELL; WILLIAM PERKIN.
WWW.MSIM.ORG.UK

N

NASMYTH, JAMES (1808–1890)
Scottish engineer who started in business in Manchester in 1834, and in 1836 established the Bridgewater Foundry at Patricroft. He invented and patented the steam hammer in 1839 and he also developed a steam pile driver. In 1858 he wrote *Remarks on Tools and Machinery*.
CHAMBERS BIOGRAPHICAL DICTIONARY.

NEW MILL
Ancoats. Built in 1806 by McConnell and Kennedy, this mill had eight floors and gas lighting was installed in 1809 by Boulton and Watt.
ROBINA MCNEIL AND MICHAEL NEVELL, *A GUIDE TO THE INDUSTRIAL ARCHAEOLOGY OF GREATER MANCHESTER* (2000); MIKE WILLIAMS WITH D A FARNIE, *COTTON MILLS IN GREATER MANCHESTER* (1992).

NEWTON HEATH
In former times a heath stretched from Miles Platting to Failsworth near Oldham and Newton Heath was a village which grew up on the heath. There were four gateways onto the Heath: Culcheth Gate, Cheetham's Gate, Dean's Gate and Greaves Gate; and four hamlets whose inhabitants lived around four village greens: Goose Green, Hobson's Green, Botany Green and Crown Point Green. A corn mill used to stand by the River Medlock, close to Clayton Bridge. In 1757 a mob rioted and attacked the mill after hearing rumours that the miller was adding ground human bones to his flour.

Farming was the main industry and the community carried on ancient traditions such as 'a-Maying' and rushbearing (on the old Celtic festival of Lughnasa in August). There was a strong belief in witchcraft and the logo of Newton Heath Traction Maintenance Depot was a witch in a pointed hat riding her broomstick. The football team of the company was initially known as The Heathens, partly because of the name Heath and partly because of the witch logo. In 1902 the team changed their name to Manchester United.

The building of the Rochdale Canal in 1804 transformed the cottage industry of linen weaving and bleaching along the banks of the Medlock. Previously linen was laid out to dry in the fields after bleaching and anyone caught stealing it paid the supreme penalty, as 18-year-old James Holland discovered to his cost in 1798. He was publicly executed in Newton Heath as a deterrent to others. Cotton spinning and silk, cotton and linen weaving mills covered the banks of the Medlock and the Rochdale Canal. Tootal Mens Wear started business in 1799 on Ten Acres Lane. There was also Sankeys Soap Works, Cardwell's Rope Works, a match factory, engineering and glass works. The Newton Heath engineering firm Heenan and Froude built Blackpool Tower 1890–4. In the 1840s the railways came and in 1877 the engine repair sheds and carriage works of Newton Heath Traction Maintenance Depot were built. Employees could take their own food to the staff canteen to be cooked for their lunch by the serving staff.

☛ *See also* MANCHESTER UNITED FOOTBALL CLUB.

GLYNIS COOPER, THE ILLUSTRATED HISTORY OF THE MANCHESTER SUBURBS (2002); NEWTON HEATH HISTORICAL SOCIETY, LOOKING BACK AT NEWTON HEATH (1993).

NICO DITCH

The Nico Ditch, also known as the Mickle or Great Ditch, runs from Ashton Moss (approximately from where the M60 motorway and interchange is built) through Gorton, Levenshulme, Longsight, Fallowfield, Rusholme and Platt Fields to Hough Moss. The Ditch was built c.870–900 and according to the Victorians ran for 5 miles 183 yards (c.9km). Most of the ditch has now disappeared under farmland and building but where it is still visible (in parts of Gorton and Platt Fields in Rusholme) it appears to be some five to six feet (about 1.75m) deep. It is an impressive feature and is supposed to have been constructed to repel the Danes during the Viking invasions.

WWW.GMAU.ORG; WWW.ART.MAN.AC.UK/FIELDARCHAEOLOGYCENTRE; WWW.MAP.TWENTYTHREE.US/NICO.HTML

NORMAN MANCHESTER

In 1066 William of Normandy invaded and conquered England. It was the final conquest for England has not been invaded since. William gave Manchester and the lands around the town to Roger of Poitou who then gave

the manor of Manchester to Sir Nigellus, a Norman knight. The town became a barony and in 1086 came into the possession of the de Grelly family in whose hands it remained until 1309. St Mary's Church received a brief mention in the Domesday Book of 1086.
WWW.MANCHESTER2002-UK.COM

NORTHENDEN
Originally Northenden lay by a crossing point on the other side of the River Mersey in Cheshire on an ancient salter's way. The river was at its shallowest here between Didsbury and Northenden. There was a ferry known as Jackson's Boat, worked by ropes, until a footbridge was built across the Mersey in the 1870s. A corn mill stood nearby in the 14th century, powered from a weir on the Mersey. Both mill and weir were demolished in the 1960s. Two medieval 'cruck construction' cottages became listed buildings in 1982 but were demolished the following day. In 1873 the 15th-century church was rebuilt by Joseph Crowther, the architect who restored Manchester Cathedral. Farming was the main means of livelihood but during the Industrial Revolution the local cottage industry of spinning flax suffered a marked decline. Northenden escaped the clutches of the millscapes and retained something of its rural charm. As late as 1930 Princess Parkway was a beautiful woodland area with cultivated fields and colourful beds of flowers. However the suburb's nemesis was the building of the neighbouring garden city of Wythenshawe and for over thirty years Northenden was swamped until Wythenshawe gained its own educational, religious, health, commercial and entertainment facilities. The whole area became part of the Mersey Valley Park during the 1980s.
GLYNIS COOPER, *THE ILLUSTRATED HISTORY OF THE MANCHESTER SUBURBS* (2002); DERRICK DEACON, *NORTHENDEN* (1983).

NORTHERN QUARTER
The term is a modern misnomer and does not mean the northern quarter of the city; but rather an area to the north of the city centre, bounded by Oldham St, Swan St, Shude Hill, Withy Grove and High St, which has reinvented itself. In 1844 Friedrich Engels condemned the whole area because 'even the better streets are tortuous and narrow ... the houses are dirty, old and tumbledown ... the side streets have been built in a disgraceful fashion'. Tib St, which runs from Debenhams store to Swan St, along with neighbouring Thomas St, is taking part in the innovative and colourful Northern Artworks Scheme. There are music shops and clothes shops and jewellery workshops with a bohemian theme, a craft centre, cheap and tasty wholefood cafes, the new Chinese arts centre; luxury residential apartments in the old fish markets; the Printworks which lies at the heart of Manchester's

Mural on Tib St reflecting the history of the street.

'vibrant and volatile' club scene; and the ever present sense of history just around the corner.

GLYNIS COOPER, *HIDDEN MANCHESTER* (2004); WWW.MANCHESTER2002-UK.COM

NORTH MANCHESTER REGENERATION

Improvement work in Newton Heath, Harpurhey, Lightbowne, Monsall. ALAN KIDD, *HISTORY OF MANCHESTER* (3RD EDN, 2002); WWW.MANCHESTER 2002-UK.COM

NORTH WEST FILM ARCHIVE

The North West Film Archive (NWFA) is a public regional collection which holds over 26,500 reels of film and videotape from early 'animated pictures' to contemporary productions, 'the experiences and interests of North West people are vividly captured in both professional and amateur footage'. The NWFA provides an unparalleled view of life in the millscapes through a collection which includes

cinema newsreels, documentaries, educational and training films, travelogues, advertising and promotional material, corporate videos and regional television programmes – alongside hundreds of films shot by local families and enthusiasts …

WWW.NWFA.MMU.AC.UK

O

OLDHAM STREET
This runs from Piccadilly to New Cross: once a fashionable commercial thoroughfare; then a street which specialized in music and craft shops; now somewhat shabby.

OLD MILL
Henry St, Ancoats. Built in 1799 for James McConnell and John Kennedy, originally textile machine manufacturers who had interests in weaving. The mill was rebuilt as Royal Mill in 1912.
ROBINA MCNEIL AND MICHAEL NEVELL, *A GUIDE TO THE INDUSTRIAL ARCHAEOLOGY OF GREATER MANCHESTER* (2000); MIKE WILLIAMS WITH D A FARNIE, *COTTON MILLS IN GREATER MANCHESTER* (1992).

OLD MILLGATE
This used to run from St Mary's Gate to Hanging Bridge, close to which was another corn mill, but it is now subsumed in Exchange St and Exchange Square.

Exchange St on the former site of Old Millgate.

The reference library in the old town hall in King St.

OLD TOWN HALL

King St. The Old Town Hall was built at the junction of King St and Cross St in 1825. It had a fine wide four-pillared porticoed entrance; the steps and entrance from King St were added in 1838. In 1878 the building became the Free Reference Library. It was demolished in 1912; the pillared and porticoed entrance was preserved and today it stands in Heaton Park on the edge of Blackley.

WWW.GMCRO.CO.UK

OLD WELLINGTON INN

The inn is a three-storey black and white timbered and gabled building with mullion style windows. Steep crooked stairs lead from the main bar to a warren of small rooms ideal for quiet or intimate meetings. The building existed in 1552, though not in its present location off Exchange Square, but in the Old Shambles. In 1554 it was purchased, together with the present Sinclairs Oyster Bar, by the Byrom family. The ground floor was then used as a linen draper's shop. John Byrom was born on 29 February 1692 in the building. He invented a system of phonetic shorthand, a forerunner of the

The Old Shambles in its original setting, c.1910; Sinclairs Oyster Bar is to the right of the Old Wellington Inn.

modern Pitman's shorthand, and made his living by teaching shorthand. He was an accomplished poet and linguist who wrote the hymn 'Christians Awake!', which he sang to his wife outside her bedroom window one Christmas morning in the 1750s.

The Old Wellington Inn has been a hostelry since 1830 when the first licence was obtained; but it was called the Vintners Arms and then Kenyon's Vaults before the ground floor was established as the Wellington Inn in 1865 while the upper floors housed mathematical and optical instrument makers. In 1897 the upper floors were taken over by the Olde Fyshing Tackle Shop. After the IRA bomb explosion in 1996 the inn was moved to its present site.

GLYNIS COOPER, *HIDDEN MANCHESTER* (2003).

OPENSHAW

Openshaw is first mentioned in 1282 as open woodland in which the king and local nobility hunted deer and wild boar. Sheep and the warships required by successive Tudor monarchs took their toll on the trees but

Openshaw was still a farming area in the 18th century. A cottage industry of bleaching had grown up as a way of supplementing income. Proximity to the millscapes of Ancoats and Ardwick and to the Ashton Canal transformed Openshaw in the Industrial Revolution. Engineering works and gun manufacture replaced farming and bleaching. Beyer Peacock locomotive builders occupied a twelve acre site on the Gorton/Openshaw border and employed hundreds of workers. Between 1821 and 1881 the population of Openshaw multiplied 32.5 times from 497 to 16,153. There were a half-dozen theatres and cinemas and many public houses, causing moral thunderings by the *Gorton and Openshaw Reporter*. The closing of the Armstrong Whitworth gun works after the First World War threw nearly 11,000 people out of work from the population of 30,000. Openshaw never really recovered. Today, however, the suburb is part of the East Manchester Regeneration Scheme and is benefiting from new building and new businesses.

GLYNIS COOPER, *THE ILLUSTRATED HISTORY OF THE MANCHESTER SUBURBS* (2002).

OPERA HOUSE

Built on Quay St in 1912, not far from the former quay, the Opera House is one of Manchester's main theatrical venues for opera, dance and musicals. When the theatre opened on Boxing Day in 1912 it was known as the New Theatre, changing its name to the New Queens in 1917. In 1930 the name of the theatre was changed again to its present name of the Opera House. The theatre can seat an audience of 2,000 people and has hosted shows such as *My Fair Lady*, *South Pacific* and *Phantom of the Opera*. Stars who have trodden the boards at the Opera House include Sir John Gielgud, Peter Ustinov, Vivienne Leigh and Sir Alec Guinness.

WWW.MANCHESTER2002-UK.COM

OWEN, ROBERT (1771–1858)

Welsh-born Robert Owen left home while he was still a child and worked in London and Stamford before working in a drapery shop on St Ann's Square. By the age of 20 he was a factory manager. Later he set up his own business enterprise, the Chorlton Twist Company. He lived at Chorlton Hall in Greenheys, the former home of Thomas de Quincy. Owen was also a member of the Manchester Literary and Philosophical Society and it was here he met Thomas Percival who helped him to clarify his emerging ideas on socialism and a more humane order. Owen published books on socialist policies and plans for setting up 'villages of co-operation', a sort of worker's co-operative backed by government funding to help the poor; but he was ahead of his time. In 1799 he married the daughter of David Dale, a philanthropist who

owned mills in New Lanark of which Owen became manager and part owner. A statue to Robert Owen stands close to Victoria Station beside the Metrolink tramlines. Owen owned mills in Manchester as well and led the fight for acceptance of the Ten Hours Bill (limiting legal working hours to ten per day) and a reduction in the hours of children working in the mills. He earned himself a good deal of unpopularity among his peers but the Bill was finally passed in 1858. Owen put some of his socialist theories into practice in his Scottish mills but after he retired from Scotland in 1828 he spent the rest of his life in promoting 'secularistic, socialistic and spiritualistic propagandism'.
CHAMBERS BIOGRAPHICAL DICTIONARY; WWW.MANCHESTER2002-UK.COM

OXFORD ROAD
This runs from Oxford St towards Rusholme. Manchester Victoria and Manchester Metropolitan universities, Manchester Museum, the Royal Northern College of Music, the Medical School, the Contact Theatre and the Holy Name Church stand on Oxford Rd.
☛ *See also* HOLY NAME CHURCH; MANCHESTER UNIVERSITY.

OXFORD ROAD TWIST MILL
Chorlton-on-Medlock. Cotton spinning mill built by Samuel Marsland in 1803 which formed part of the Chorlton Mills complex. The mill was demolished *c.*1930.
ROBINA MCNEIL AND MICHAEL NEVELL, *A GUIDE TO THE INDUSTRIAL ARCHAEOLOGY OF GREATER MANCHESTER* (2000); MIKE WILLIAMS WITH D A FARNIE, *COTTON MILLS IN GREATER MANCHESTER* (1992).

OXFORD STREET
This runs south from St Peter's Square to Oxford Rd and boasts a multiscreen cinema complex.

OX (FORMERLY THE OXNOBLE) HOTEL
Liverpool Rd. The oxnoble was a type of potato popular in Victorian England. Barrow boys, known as the oxnoble men, unloaded these potatoes at the potato wharf in nearby Castlefield, and this traditional pub was one of their favourite watering holes. Local painters display their work on the walls and local bands play blues music.
WWW.MANCHESTER2002-UK.COM

P

PALACE THEATRE
Oxford Road. This opened on 18 May 1891 with a performance of the ballet *Cleopatra*. In the earlier part of the 20th century, artists who performed there included Laurel and Hardy, Danny Kaye, Gracie Fields, Charles Laughton, Judy Garland, and Noel Coward. In more recent times the theatre has become a venue for big musicals such as *Les Miserables, Cats* and *Miss Saigon*.
WWW.MANCHESTER2002-UK.COM

PANKHURST, CHRISTABEL (1880–1958)
The elder daughter of Richard and Emmeline Pankhurst she trained in law and was the first woman to be awarded a Bachelor of Law degree from the Victoria University of Manchester. However, being a woman, she was refused entry to Lincoln's Inn and she had difficulty finding work. She persuaded her mother to found the Women's Social and Political Union and marked the beginning of militant campaigning for women's suffrage by demonstrating at a meeting held in the Free Trade Hall. She was arrested for refusing to pay the subsequent fine. After universal suffrage was finally granted in 1928, she left England to live in British Columbia in Canada where she preached Christ's Second Coming and became an evangelist in the Second Advent Church. She was made a dame in 1936.
CHAMBERS BIOGRAPHICAL DICTIONARY.

PANKHURST, EMMELINE (1858–1928)
She was born in Manchester, the daughter of Robert Goulden, a calico printer. She married a barrister, Richard Pankhurst, in 1879, who championed women's rights and she campaigned with him for women's suffrage and acceptance of the Married Women's Property Act. They lived at 62 Nelson St, on the border of Longsight and Chorlton-on-Medlock, and had two daughters: Christabel (1880–1958) and Sylvia (1882-1960). After Richard died in 1898 Emmeline worked for the Registrar of Births and Deaths in Rusholme until 1907. She campaigned tirelessly for the vote for women and, with another suffragette, Annie Kenney, she founded the Women's Social and Political Union in 1905 which used violent means to fight for women's suffrage. Emmeline was frequently imprisoned but each time she went on hunger strike and was usually quickly released. The First World War saw the tide change and in 1918 women over 30 were given the vote as a reward for having done all the work traditionally done by men while the men were away fighting. She lived long enough to see universal suffrage granted in 1928. She also worked hard to reform conditions in the workhouses.
CHAMBERS BIOGRAPHICAL DICTIONARY.

PANKHURST, SYLVIA (1882–1960)

Sylvia, the younger daughter of Richard and Emmeline Pankhurst, did not have the same high profile as her mother and sister, though she worked hard to support the campaign for women's suffrage. During the 1890s she sometimes accompanied her father when he was campaigning for the Independent Labour Party and she saw at first hand the desperation of life for the mill workers. She wrote:

> often I went on Sunday mornings with my father to the dingy streets of Ancoats, Gorton, Hulme, and other working-class districts … those endless rows of smoke-begrimed little houses, with never a tree or a flower in sight, how bitterly their ugliness smote me! Many a time in spring, as I gazed upon them, those two red may trees in our garden at home would rise up in my mind, almost menacing in their beauty; and I would ask myself whether it could be just that I should live in Victoria Park, and go well fed and warmly clad, whilst the children of these grey slums were lacking the very necessities of life.

After 1928, when the right to vote was given to all women, Sylvia diverged into pacifism, internationalism and socialist politics; and she wrote a biography of her mother in 1935.
CHAMBERS BIOGRAPHICAL DICTIONARY.

PARAGON MILL

Ancoats. Built in 1912 by Manchester Fine Spinners on the same lines as the Royal Mill.
ROBINA MCNEIL AND MICHAEL NEVELL, *A GUIDE TO THE INDUSTRIAL ARCHAEOLOGY OF GREATER MANCHESTER* (2000); MIKE WILLIAMS WITH D A FARNIE, *COTTON MILLS IN GREATER MANCHESTER* (1992).

PAWNBROKERS

Pawnbrokers, like Robert Furlong of Cheetham Hill, used to be a very common sight in 19th- and early 20th-century Manchester. The poorest families would receive their meagre wages on a Friday but by Monday the money was usually all gone. Wives and mothers would queue to pawn their wedding rings, their husband's suits, their household goods, anything for which they might get the loan of a few pence to put food on the table for their families. Their possessions would be redeemed and retrieved on Friday night only to be back in pawn again by Monday morning. There are still pawnbrokers in Manchester, especially around the Cross St area, but these are discreetly tucked away. The age of credit cards has made cash and goods generally much easier to acquire but often at a much higher rate of interest than the pawnbrokers would charge.

The tradition of pawnbroking can be traced back at least 3,000 years to China and it was known to the ancient Greek and Roman civilizations as well. In medieval times the Church prohibited the charging of interest on loans so pawnbrokers tended to be of non-Christian beliefs. The three golden balls, symbol of pawnbrokers, were part of the Medici coat of arms, the ruling Italian family who became almost synonymous with the finance and loans industry of the 15th century and who established the Medici banking empire in Florence. A weasel is a shoemaker's tool and 'pop' is to pawn hence the lines of the nursery rhyme:

A penny for a spool of thread
A penny for a needle,
That's the way the money goes,
Pop! Goes the weasel.

A half a pound of tuppenny rice,
A half a pound of treacle.
Mix it up and make it nice,
Pop! Goes the weasel.

Up and down the London road,
In and out of the Eagle,
That's the way the money goes,
Pop! Goes the weasel.

I've no time to plead and pine,
I've no time to wheedle,
Kiss me quick and then I'm gone
Pop! Goes the weasel.

WWW.EXCASHOFPANAMACITY.COM/HISTORY2.HTM

PEACE, CHARLES (D. 1876)

Charles Peace was a petty burglar who believed that he was irresistible to women. The reality was that he was lame, tight-lipped and had an ugly squat nose. On 1 August 1876, a warm summer afternoon, he had gone out to Chorlton-cum-Hardy with the intention of burgling Darley Hall that evening. He aroused the suspicions of PC Nicholas Cock who was on street patrol duty that day. PC Cock, a local 'neighbourhood bobby', had a reputation for being zealous, to excess sometimes, so he followed Peace and challenged him. Charles Peace panicked and shot PC Cock at point blank range in the chest before fleeing the scene. PC Cock later died from his injuries and was buried in the parish church by the village green. Two local brothers, who were farm workers and who were known to have a grudge against PC Cock, were charged with the crime. One was tried and found guilty but unusually he did not receive the death sentence. This was fortunate as he turned out to be innocent. Charles Peace was eventually arrested for some other misdemeanour and confessed to the killing.

Glynis Cooper, *The Illustrated History of the Manchester Suburbs* (2002); John Lloyd, *Looking Back at Chorlton-cum-Hardy* (1985).

PEOPLE'S HISTORY MUSEUM

103 Princess Street. Built by the architect John Gregan in the warehouse 'palazzo style' in 1854, this red-brick three-storey building, with a basement and an attic hidden behind a balustrade, giving the place a warehouse appearance, was intended to be a 'centre of learning and education for the educable working classes'. It was replacing the Mechanics Institute premises in Cooper St, used since 1825, which were now too small for the numbers wishing to study English, maths, languages and music. Subsequently it became Museum of Labour History, which has now moved to the Pumphouse, and today the building is the People's History Museum and includes a large trade union archive.

WWW.MANCHESTER2002-UK.COM

PERKIN, SIR WILLIAM HENRY (1838–1907)

Chemist who lived in Manchester for a time and discovered artificial aniline dyes in 1856. Purple was the first such dye to be manufactured. His son, William, became Professor of Chemistry at Manchester University in 1892. Perkin's original notebooks are held by the Museum of Science and Industry.

WWW.SPINNINGTHEWEB.ORG.UK

PERRY, FRED (1909–1995)

Born in Stockport, Greater Manchester, Fred Perry was possibly the best tennis player that England has ever produced. He was three times Wimbledon Champion (1934–6); the first player to win all four Grand Slam singles titles and the last Englishman to win the All England men's title. He also won three American, one Australian and one French title. As a child he played table tennis and did not train for lawn tennis until he was 18. He could deliver very fast backhanders. Perry brought the Davis Cup to England three times (1934–6). After his playing career he became a tennis commentator and writer. He was elected to the Wimbledon Hall of Fame in 1975.

WWW.MANCHESTER2002-UK.COM

PETERLOO MASSACRE 1819

The Peterloo Massacre took place in St Peter's Fields in Manchester on 16 August 1819. It was given the name by an eye witness who had fought at Waterloo a few years earlier because the aftermath resembled a battlefield with dead and injured lying everywhere.

St Peter's Fields covered an area which today includes Peter St, the Midland Hotel, the GMEX, the Free Trade Hall and Central Library. A public meeting had been arranged on that Sunday at which several speakers, including Henry Hunt, Richard Carlile and Samuel Bamford, would address an audience on unfair working practices, the need for reform and radical ideas for the way forward; or in the jargon of the day, 'calling for reforms to conditions which condemned thousands to a life of poverty, wretchedness, tyranny and injustice'.

By lunchtime the crowd was some 80,000 strong. The mood was good-natured. Many had walked a long way to hear the speakers but they were mostly families dressed in their Sunday best for a day out. The magistrates were nervous however. It was barely thirty years since the French Revolution and the authorities were nervous of civil unrest. They ordered 1,200 cavalry, several hundred infantry and 400 special constables to be on duty in case of disorder.

At about 1.30pm nerves finally took over from common sense and William Hulton, chairman of the magistrates, ordered the arrest of the speakers and the cavalry to disperse the crowd. The cavalry, knowing they were heavily outnumbered, decided on charge and slash tactics rather than peaceful means of dispersal. Accordingly they charged into the crowd, slashing wildly to the right and left with their sabres. Total panic ensued. Within ten minutes St Peter's Fields were empty except for twenty men, women and children who had been killed and 400 people who were lying injured.

The speakers were arrested, the magistrates were congratulated and the Government, failing to suppress news of the massacre, carried out a 'whitewashing' exercise. Although controversy raged about exactly what had happened there was some admission of corporate guilt and compensation was paid to those injured and to the families of those who had been killed. John Rylands Library on Deansgate holds the original death and injuries compensation book for Peterloo. Compiled in 1820 the book details the names, ages and addresses of those who died or were injured, the injuries they received and the amount of compensation paid.

The ordinary working people of Manchester never forgot or forgave Peterloo and for over 150 years afterwards the sight of mounted uniforms in Manchester gave rise to intense public unease.

WWW.SPARTACUS.SCHOOLNET.CO.UK; WWW.COTTONTIMES.CO.UK;
WWW.SPINNINGTHEWEB.ORG.UK

PETER STREET
This runs from St Peter's Square to Deansgate and was part of the site of the Peterloo Massacre in 1819. The Midland Hotel and the Free Trade Hall stand on Peter St.

PHILIPS PARK
Bradford. Mark Philips, one of the first two MPs for Manchester after the 1832 Reform Act, established Philips Park in 1846. Public parks were one of his enthusiasms because he recognized the need for workers to have somewhere pleasant to spend their few leisure hours. Philips Park covered 30 acres and included flowerbeds, glasshouses and a lake. Some, however, felt that the large cemetery across the River Medlock opposite the park made Philips Park an oppressive place.
WWW.MANCHESTER2003-UK.COM

PICCADILLY
This runs from Piccadilly Gardens and the bus station to Piccadilly Railway Station where it joins London Rd.

Metrolink leaving Piccadilly for Bury.

PICCADILLY GARDENS

A former clay pit, the land for the gardens was donated to Manchester by Lord Mosley in the 18th century on the condition that it should always be for public use. The Royal Infirmary stood on the west side (where the Piccadilly Hotel stands today) and a large oval pond was built on the land in front of the hospital and landscaped to provide an enjoyable view for patients. After the infirmary was moved in 1908 the pond was drained and it was this that gave Piccadilly Gardens their sunken effect. A bus and tram terminus grew up around the gardens which were a good central vantage point. During the Second World War the Gardens were given over to allotments for growing food according to the dictates of the wartime government.

During the 1950 and 1960s the gardens were renovated with lawns and flowerbeds and flowering cherry trees which gave a brief riotous blaze of pink and white blossoms each springtime. Statues of Queen Victoria, the Duke of Wellington, Sir Robert Peel and James Watt stood around the periphery.

In 1999 Piccadilly Gardens were redeveloped and a third of the area lost under the building of a new six-storey office block. There is an oval fountain, which only works for part of the time, and formal lawns, backed by a plain grim concrete wall. The colour and the character and the beautiful flowering

Concrete wall with the Cow Trail along the top at Piccadilly Gardens.

cherry trees have gone; and the bus station seems to have expanded with a bewildering number of different services.
WWW.MANCHESTERONLINE.CO.UK

PICCADILLY RADIO

261 FM, Piccadilly Plaza. Started out in the 1970s as Manchester's first independent local radio station broadcasting music, local and national news; well known for its presenters.
WWW.NORTHWESTRADIO.INFO

PICCADILLY STATION

London Rd. The original name of Piccadilly Station was Store St, which now runs beneath the station following the route of the long disappeared Shooter's Brook. The Duke of Bridgewater's 'lost canal' ran from Castlefield to a point just below the present Station Approach. Store St station opened in 1842 and was the terminus for the London and Birmingham Railway. The Manchester, Sheffield and Lincolnshire railway became operational in 1845 and also worked from Store St station. The two companies rebuilt the station in 1865 and renamed it London Rd. Mayfield Goods Station stood adjacent to the passenger station and the remains of this station can still be seen

Metrolink Cow on the Cow Trail, Piccadilly Station.

Piccadilly Station, showing restored station roof.

alongside the two through lines on the southern side of Piccadilly. London
Rd was renamed Piccadilly during the latter part of the 20th century. Today
it is the main station for London services, Scottish expresses and trains to the
south of England.

ALAN KIDD, *HISTORY OF MANCHESTER* (3RD EDN, 2002); WWW.MANCHESTER
2002-UK.COM

PICKLES BUILDING

This warehouse stands at 101 Princess St, adjacent to the People's History Museum. Designed by Clegg & Knowles 1858–63 in 'palazzo' style, it is now the Princess Hotel.

SIMON TAYLOR ET AL., *MANCHESTER: THE WAREHOUSE LEGACY* (2002).

PLATT FIELDS

Rusholme. Platt Fields were originally held by the Knights Hospitallers of St John of Jerusalem in the 12th century. Today they form the grounds of Platt Hall, now a costume museum. A statue of Abraham Lincoln stood near the house until 1986 when it was removed to Lincoln Square near the Town Hall. Platt Unitarian Chapel still stands in the grounds. Despite their proximity to the bustling Wilmslow Rd, Platt Fields still retain the peace and tranquillity of earlier centuries.

☛ *See also PLATT HALL MUSEUM OF COSTUME.*

WWW.MANCHESTER2003-UK.COM

PLATT HALL MUSEUM OF COSTUME

Platt Hall lies in Platt Fields off Wilmslow Rd on the Rusholme/ Fallowfield borders and on the No. 42 bus route to Didsbury. The original hall was a medieval black and white timbered building but the present house only dates from the 1760s. The hall was the seat of the Worsleys who were staunch Parliamentarians during the Civil War (1640–9) and personal friends of Oliver Cromwell. When Cromwell took the mace from the House of Commons he ordered it to be kept at Platt Hall for three months.

The present Platt Hall is a three-storey red brick Georgian building of graceful proportions, with the main staircase sweeping up from a spacious entrance. It houses one of the largest collections in the country of men, women and children's costumes dating from 1600 to 1990. Costume galleries and themed exhibitions occupy the ground and first floors, while the library and costume archives are on the second floor. The former servant's rooms in the attics are used for the storage of babies' garments, women's bonnets, men and women's silken stockings.

Treasures include a dainty pet-en-lair jacket said to have belonged to the wife of the famous 18th-century actor, David Garrick, and a banyan (formal dressing gown) given by George III to his Lord Chamberlain. Among the curiosities are combinations, corsets (and descriptions of how to wear them), and a pretty pair of blue and white stockings knitted by a Westphalian girl for her wedding in the 1840s.

WWW.MANCHESTER2002-UK.COM; WWW.SPINNINGTHEWEB.ORG.UK

PLUG PLOTS 1842

A series of strikes took place in which mills were forced to stop working by the removal of plugs from the boilers which steam-powered the machinery. These strikes were caused by reductions in wages and by the demands of the Chartists which included the universal male right to vote, secret ballots, annual elections; constituencies of equal population size, payments of MPs and the abolition of a minimum property requirement for MPs. The strikes did not achieve their aims and the Chartist Movement declined, although today all its demands have been realized except for annual elections.
WWW.SPINNINGTHEWEB.ORG.UK

POOL FOLD HALL

Cross St. This moated manor house was built in the 14th century by the Radcliffes and stood partly in Cross St, partly in Pall Mall, halfway down the slope from Browne St to Cross St. A memory of it is preserved in the name Back Pool Fold, a lane off Cross St. There is a description of the hall from the 1770s:

> a large timber structure with its heavy portico of wood and its massy and projecting chimney place of stone presents itself ... from Market Street Lane ... it was built near the foot of a knoll and encircled by a moat ... the gardens and orchard were spanned by a drawbridge in the Avenue [now Cross St/Newmarket Place] from the Pool gates [opposite Corporation St] to the portico ...

The hall was demolished in 1781 and replaced initially by the new market and then in 1810 by warehouses.
LANCASHIRE RECORD OFFICE, *NEWSPAPER CUTTINGS OF MANCHESTER AND SALFORD* (*C*.1908).

POPULATION

Manchester has thirty suburbs clustered around the nucleus of the City Centre. The table lists their respective number of residents. The total population of Manchester city and suburbs is currently *c.* 430,000.
MANCHESTER WARD PROFILES IN LOCAL STUDIES DEPT CENTRAL LIBRARY.

Ancoats	included in original city in 1838	*c.*2,500
Ardwick	included in original city in 1838	10,700
Beswick	included in original city in 1838	*c.*4,000
Blackley	incorporated 1890 (Heaton park 1903)	11,500
Bradford	incorporated 1885	*c.*10,600
Burnage	incorporated 1904	14,000

Cheetham	included in original city in 1838	16,000
Chorlton-cum-Hardy	incorporated 1904	14,000
Chorlton-on-Medlock	included in original city in 1838	*c*.7,000
Clayton	incorporated 1890	*c*.6,300
Collyhurst	incorporated 1885	12,500
Crumpsall	incorporated 1890	13,000
Didsbury	incorporated 1904	14,500
Fallowfield	incorporated 1895 (nth part, sth part 1904)	15,000
Gorton	incorporated W. Gorton 1890, Gorton 1909	26,000
Harpurhey	incorporated 1885	11,000
Hulme	included in original city in 1838	9,700
Levenshulme	incorporated 1909	13,000
Longsight	incorporated 1890	16,500
Miles Platting	included in original city in 1838	*c*.5,000
Moss Side	incorporated 1904	11,700
Moston	incorporated 1890	12,500
Newton Heath	incorporated 1890	12,500
Northenden	incorporated 1931	12,500
Openshaw	incorporated 1890	*c*.9,000
Rusholme	incorporated 1885	16,000
Victoria Park	incorporated 1885	*c*.2,000
Whalley Range	incorporated 1904	13,000
Withington/Ladybarn	incorporated 1904	14,000
Wythenshawe	incorporated 1931	100,000

PORTICO LIBRARY

Mosley St/Charlotte St. The library is housed in an elegant porticoed building. It opened in 1806 as a subscription library and newsroom and was run like a private club for commercial and professional men. Today the Mosley St frontage has been taken over by another business and the entrance is from Charlotte St, close to Gibbs Bookshop. The Portico is still a subscription library and membership is dependent upon personal recommendation. Inside the style is still reminiscent of a club from another era; very quiet and secluded among the tall bookshelves and galleries and with the aroma of old-fashioned home-cooked lunches wafting from the dining room.

WWW.MANCHESTERONLINE.CO.UK

PORTLAND STREET

This runs from Piccadilly to Oxford St and formed part of the warehouse complex which lay at the commercial heart of the city. A number of warehouses still survive which have been converted to other uses; most notably the former S & H WATTS WAREHOUSE which is now the Britannia Hotel.

POWELL, ROBERT (B. 1944)

He was born in Salford just across the Irwell from Manchester and educated at Manchester Grammar School. He began his career in repertory theatre and made his screen debut in 1967. Stardom came with his role as Mahler in Ken Russell's film of that name and playing Jesus in Franco Zefirelli's *Jesus of Nazareth*. He has also appeared in several other films including *The Italian Job* and *The Thirty Nine Steps*.

WWW.MANCHESTER2002-UK.COM

POTTER, EDMUND (1802–1879)

Grandfather of internationally acclaimed children's writer Beatrix Potter. Born in Ardwick Green in 1802, one of two surviving children of James and Mary Potter. James Potter was a merchant. His wife Jessie came from Lancaster's mayoral family. Edmund Potter was a self-made man who developed innovative methods of textile printing and owned the largest calico printing business in the world at Dinting Vale near Glossop. He took over Cobden's warehouse at 14–16 Mosley St which is today home to Lloyd's Bank. Edmund Potter also wrote a number of pamphlets on various subjects and eventually became MP for Carlisle.

GLYNIS REEVE, *A NORTH COUNTRY LASS* ... (2001).

PREHISTORIC MANCHESTER

Stone Age and Bronze Age peoples left behind their stone, flint and bronze tools, weapons and jewellery on the banks of Manchester streams and rivers but it wasn't until the coming of the Celts during the Iron Age that there was any proper and lasting settlement of Manchester.

GLYNIS COOPER, *THE ILLUSTRATED HISTORY OF THE MANCHESTER SUBURBS* (2002).

PRINTWORKS

Withy Grove. Formerly the Withy Grove Press which was the largest press plant in Europe. Taken over by Robert Maxwell in the early 1980s and renamed Maxwell House. The *Daily Mirror* was printed here until 1986. By 1987 the Printworks was closed and derelict; but it was restored and transformed under an urban regeneration scheme after the IRA bomb blast of 1996. Today the Printworks is like a small enclosed village of cafe society. There are pavement bars and cafes like Norwegian Blue and Hard Rock Cafe; pubs and clubs such as Babushka and Tiger! Tiger!, a twenty-screen cinema complex (The Filmworks); the Hard Rock Casino; a bookshop, designer shops and a health club. The Printworks lies at the heart of Manchester's club scene.

GLYNIS COOPER, *HIDDEN MANCHESTER* (2004).

Q

QUARRY BANK MILL

Quarry Bank Mill was built by Samuel Greg in 1784 on the edge of Styal village about 2 miles from the outer Manchester suburb of Wythenshawe. The Gregs had a number of mills in the Greater Manchester area. Quarry Bank was an early mill and it had an apprentice house which still survives. Two-thirds of the workforce at Quarry Bank Mill were children, often taken from the local workhouses, and, as the mill was situated among green fields in the countryside by the River Bollin and some distance from the town, Greg built an apprentice house to accommodate them.

Samuel Greg was one of the more humanitarian mill owners, although the children's living conditions appear spartan by modern standards. Porridge formed a large part of their staple diet but the children were given bread and fresh vegetables once a day and often they had meat on Sundays. There was a schoolroom where the children received a basic education after they had finished work. They did not work nights and their daily hours from 6 a.m. to 6 p.m. were considered quite moderate. The children slept two to a bed in small truckle beds ranged in rows. There was also a surgery in the house and a local doctor, retained by Samuel Greg to care for the children, called in regularly, often several times a week.

The apprentice system had declined by the 1840s and the apprentice house closed in 1845. It is now a museum of living history where 21st-century children can learn through a 'hands-on' experience how their 19th-century counterparts lived, worked and received an education.

Quarry Bank Mill remains a working mill and visitors can see the complete process of cotton manufacture from arrival of the raw cotton through the stages of cleaning, carding, spinning, weaving, bleaching and dyeing to the finished product. Cotton calicoes manufactured at Quarry Bank Mill are on sale in the mill's Museum Shop.

WWW.QUARRYBANKMILL.ORG.UK

QUEENS PARK

Harpurhey. This park was created by Mark Philips in the grounds of Hendham Hall in 1845. One of the first two parks in Manchester, Queens Park had an art gallery and a museum. There was also a statue to Ben Brierley, a 19th-century Manchester poet and dialect writer. Hendham Hall was demolished in 1884.

WWW.MANCHESTER2003-UK.COM

R

RAFFALD, ELIZABETH (1733–1781)

Born in Doncaster, she trained as a housekeeper. She met and married gardener John Raffald at Arley House in Cheshire. They had six children and moved to Manchester in 1763. There she wrote and published *The Experienced English Housekeeper* and a book on midwifery and she also compiled a *Directory of Manchester* and the first *Registry for Servants*.
WWW.MANCHESTER2002-UK.COM

REDHILL STREET MILL

Ancoats. A spinning mill eight storeys high, built in 1818 by McConnell and Kennedy. In 1835 Alexis de Tocqueville described it as

a place where some 1500 workers, labouring 69 hours a week, with an average wage of 11 shillings, and where three-quarters of the workers are women and children …

ROBINA MCNEIL AND MICHAEL NEVELL, *A GUIDE TO THE INDUSTRIAL ARCHAEOLOGY OF GREATER MANCHESTER* (2000); MIKE WILLIAMS WITH D A FARNIE, *COTTON MILLS IN GREATER MANCHESTER* (1992).

RILEY, HAROLD (B. 1934)

Born in Salford just before Christmas in 1934 Harold Riley was a friend of L S Lowry who also acted as his mentor. He had his own show at 19 in Salford Art Gallery and attended the Slade School of Drawing for six years. Riley was a keen footballer as well and was picked to play for the Manchester United Youth Team. Faced with a career choice between art and football he eventually chose art and made his home in Salford. Like Lowry his paintings are inspired by the industrial North-West but he has also painted a number of portraits of celebrities such as Pope John Paul II, Nelson Mandela and the Duke of Edinburgh.
WWW.MANCHESTER2002-UK.COM

RISING SUN

Long Millgate. The official date given for this inn is 1612 but the black and white timbered building with its overhanging gable, which stood almost opposite the entry to Chetham's College, was much older. This public house had low ceilings, curious passages, small rooms and diamond-paned windows, according to a newspaper report in the early 1900s.

During the 1830s William Earnshaw became the licensee and renamed the pub the Sun Inn. It became popular with local poets, no doubt due to the fact that Earnshaw was something of a poet himself, and this led to the pub becoming known as Poets Corner. Informal meetings of the poetry group eventually became more formal. John Critchley, known as the Prince of Hyde, was the principal poet and John Bolton Rogerson was the secretary. In 1842–3 monthly poetical dinners were held at the Sun, the first being on 7 January 1842. A plain home-cooked meal would be followed by readings, tobacco and ale. At the March dinner it was proposed to publish a commemorative volume of poetry. This was agreed and *The Festive Wreath* appeared later that year. Contributors included J C Prince, J B Rogerson, Robert Rose, J Mill, R Story, W Gaspey, Elijah Ridings, Richard Wright Proctor, Alexander Wilson, B Stott, J Ball, J Dent, W Taylor, T A Tidmarsh, and, surprisingly, four ladies: Miss Isabella Varley, Mrs Caulton, Mrs E S Craven Green and Miss Eliza Battye.

The Rising Sun public house on Long Millgate c.1880, popularly known as Poets Corner because of the poetry dinners which took place there in the 1840s.

Change was in the air however. In 1843 John Rogerson left to take up a post as registrar at Harpurhey Cemetery. Soon afterwards, the landlord, William Earnshaw also left to work in Harpurhey; and John Critchley returned to his native Hyde. The last dinner was held early in 1843 and shortly afterwards the meetings ceased, it being said that the new landlord did not like poets or poetry.

Poets Corner was demolished in 1923 after the building had become structurally unsafe. Today the smooth green lawns and modern fountains of the Cathedral Gardens cover the site which is somewhat overshadowed by the ultramodern Urbis Museum.

LANCASHIRE RECORD OFFICE, *NEWSPAPER CUTTINGS OF MANCHESTER AND SALFORD (c.*1908).

ROADS

Manchester was an important meeting point of route ways in Roman times, which was one of the reasons for the building of the fort at Castlefield. Important saltways from the Cheshire wiches passed south-west to north-east through Northenden, along Burnage Lane and linked up with the modern A57 leading to the A628 through Longdendale and into Yorkshire. The main route to Chester lay south of Deansgate and Deansgate is said to lie along the track of a former Roman road which linked Castlefield to the Celtic settlement of Manchester where the Cathedral now stands. The old London Rd, now the A6 and the first modern 'trunk road', passed south-east through Buxton and Derby on its way from Manchester to London. Long Millgate was the main route to the north.

These roads continued in use through the medieval period and beyond and have survived into modern times, laying the foundations for the busy tangle of roads which now surround Manchester. In the last thirty years several new motorways have been built which include the M61 to Bolton and M63 to Preston; the M62 across the Pennines to Leeds; the M65 to Liverpool; the M66 around Bury; the M67 out towards Sheffield and most recently the M60 which is a circular ring road.

WWW.SPINNINGTHEWEB.ORG.UK

ROCHDALE CANAL

The Rochdale Canal from Manchester to Rochdale was completed in 1804 and this linked across the city to the Bridgewater Canal at Castlefield, creating something of a spaghetti junction of waterways. The original canal ran for 33 miles between Sowerby Bridge in West Yorkshire and Manchester.

ALAN KIDD, *HISTORY OF MANCHESTER* (3RD EDN, 2002).

Café society along the Rochdale Canal underneath railway arches near Deansgate Station.

ROGET, PETER MARK (1779–1869)

Roget came from a Swiss family who lived in London. He qualified as a doctor and published several works on consumption (tuberculosis), and wrote on the effects of the newly discovered chemical nitrous oxide (known as 'laughing gas' and a major anaesthetic). From 1804 to 1808 he worked as a surgeon in Manchester and during this time he founded the Manchester Medical School. He also lectured on medical topics, and spoke at the Literary and Philosophical Society. Roget was the first secretary at the newly formed Portico Library. After his retirement in 1840 he compiled his well-known *Thesaurus of English Words and Phrases*, first published in 1852.
CHAMBERS BIOGRAPHICAL DICTIONARY.

ROLLS-ROYCE

Frederick Royce (1863–1933) set up his first workshop in Cooke St in Hulme. He had always been interested in engineering and he began manufacturing arc lamps and dynamos. Due to foreign competition Royce decided to diversify and moved into motor car development, a subject which had begun to fascinate him, so he bought a 10 horsepower 1903 Decauville. He wanted to experiment and try to produce a better, quieter more reliable engine and in 1903 he produced his first 2 cylinder engine.

In 1904 Royce met Charles Rolls, an entrepreneur, businessman and marketing expert, in the Midland Hotel which has a plaque to commemorate the event. Rolls agreed to handle the financial and business side; Royce would produce the cars. In this way the world-renowned firm of Rolls-Royce was born.

Royce then developed one of the best known cars, the 50 horsepower 'Silver Phantom', which remained in production until 1925; followed by the 'Phantom' and the 'Wraith'. However Charles Rolls was killed in a flying accident in 1911 and Royce became ill through financial worries and overwork. He carried on and in 1915 he produced the Eagle aeroplane engine used during the rest of the First World War. During the Second World War Royce's 12 cylinder V engines were used in most fighter planes.

The Midland Hotel where Frederick Royce and Charles Rolls first met to form their historic partnership of Rolls-Royce. The hotel carries a commemorative plaque of the event.

In 1918 Frederick Royce was awarded the OBE and in 1930 he received a knighthood.

A plaque marks the site of his first workshop in Hulme.

WWW.MANCHESTER2002-UK.COM

ROMAN MANCHESTER

Agricola built the first Roman fort in AD 79 at Castlefield, where the River Medlock and the River Irwell converge 'two flyshottes' downstream from the Celtic stronghold. It was a timber and turf construction covering some five acres with two defensive ditches on three sides and the river on the fourth side. The fort was initially known as Mamuciam (mam is Celtic for a rounded hill). A larger fort was built *c.*160, followed by a stone fort of similar plan *c.*200. The name was also changed at some point to Mamceastre (from mam meaning hill and ceastre meaning walled town). Seventeen changes were

A reconstructed Roman watch tower overlooks part of the club scene.

made to the defences of Mamceastre before the Romans abandoned Britain in 410.
☛ *See also* CASTLEFIELD.
GLYNIS COOPER, *HIDDEN MANCHESTER* (2002).

ROSCOE, SIR HENRY (1833–1915)

Henry Enfield Roscoe was Professor of Chemistry at Owens College in Manchester from 1857 to 1886 and built the first ever practical chemistry laboratory in Britain. He isolated element 23, vanadium, in 1865 and in 1858 was said to have produced the world's first flashlight photograph. The commemorative Roscoe Medal is awarded for outstanding contributions to and excellence in chemistry in the UK and the Roscoe Building in the modern University of Manchester is named after him. He married Lucy Potter, an aunt of the writer Beatrix Potter.
WWW.MANCHESTER2002-UK.COM

ROVERS RETURN

The Rovers Return public house is well known to all fans of *Coronation Street* but there was a real pub named the Rovers Return which was built in 1306 and stood on Shude Hill. It was a narrow three-storey building which must have been one of the earliest surviving buildings in Manchester. Unfortunately it did not survive the redevelopments of the millscapes in the 20th century and all that is left is an old photograph locked away in the Manchester archives.
GLYNIS COOPER, *HIDDEN MANCHESTER* (2003); WWW.GMCRO.CO.UK

ROYAL EXCHANGE THEATRE

St Ann's Square. The Royal Exchange Theatre is 'a futuristic metal and glass hi-tech structure sitting inside what was described as "the biggest room in the world" – the Great Hall of Manchester's old Cotton Exchange, which ceased trading in December 1968'. The Royal Exchange was the third cotton exchange to be built; its solidity and grandeur reflecting Manchester's importance in the cotton manufacturing trade. Trading figures from the last day's trading were left in situ. The solidity of the building stood it in good stead when a large IRA bomb exploded a few yards away in 1996. Surrounding buildings had to be demolished but the infrastructure of the Exchange withstood the impact. The theatre was closed for four years but reopened in 2000. It is a theatre in-the-round, seating about 800 people around the performance area; and for those in the front banquettes at ground floor level the experience is one of being truly involved with the play and the actors.
WWW.MANCHESTER2002-UK.COM

The former Cotton Exchange, now the Royal Exchange Theatre.

RUSH CARTS

A significant part of the celebration of the original Wakes was the rush cart being paraded through the village to the church, bringing rushes to be strewn on the floor.

Samuel Bamford records in his autobiography how the practice of 'rushbearing' began, with some families bringing rushes into the church to warm their feet during the winter, eventually this grew to a tradition as the families tried to outdo each other and ingratiate themselves with the priest, and soon the whole village would be involved in preparing the cart and joining the procession to the church on the feast of the dedication; other hamlets around bringing their own gaily decorated carts, thus the village would become the focus of festivities for one day a year.

The cart would be decorated with brightly coloured rosettes, bells, flowers and silver objects borrowed from members of the congregation and displayed to show the prosperity of the village. The rushes were then piled up in a carefully constructed form, topped with waving green boughs, and sitting astride the rush-heap one or two young men of the village. In Gorton this took place at Fox Fold at the rear of the Lord Nelson public house. The whole thing was then drawn to the church, joining others from the district and forming a procession. With the church bells pealing the rushes entered the church.

WWW.SPINNINGTHEWEB.ORG.UK

RUSHOLME

Rusholme, the village of the rushes, remained just that until the late 19th century. Not mentioned in official records until 1235, the area was obviously familiar to the Romans because a hoard of around 200 Roman coins was discovered by workmen during the 1890s. The coins dated to the 3rd or 4th century and were probably buried as a precaution in some time of strife as the 'long sunset' of the Roman withdrawal from Britain began.

The Nico Ditch was built to try and repel other invaders 500 years later when the Vikings ravaged the country. Running from Ashton Moss to Hough Moss in Chorlton, part of the ditch follows the line of Old Hall Lane and Park Grove on the Levenshulme and Rusholme border. Legend says that the ditch was constructed in a single night, which must have been a night of blood, sweat, tears and blind panic.

Platt Fields, on the Wilmslow Rd, were held by the Knights Hospitallers of St John of Jerusalem in the 12th century. The first Platt Hall was a medieval black and white timbered building. The mace (or the 'bauble' as Cromwell termed it) from the House of Commons was kept here for three months in the Civil War (1640–9). Platt Hall was rebuilt in 1774 and today houses a costume museum. A statue of Abraham Lincoln stood in front of the house until 1986 when it was moved to Lincoln Square.

Birch Hall, another 16th-century building, stood on Birch Hall Lane, but together with Birch Hall Farm and Birch Fold, the hall was demolished in 1931 when the estate was sold to Manchester Grammar School for a new school to be built.

Birch Chapel was closed in 1844 because it had become too small for its congregation. Herbert Asquith, an early 20th-century Prime Minster, was married at the Congregational Church (demolished in 1978) on Wilmslow Rd in 1877. Dickenson Rd Methodist Church (formerly the Wesleyan Church) was rebuilt in 1863 in Ladybarn Lane. Two upper storeys were used as a working men's club, The church closed in 1940 but the buildings were used as film studios for making comedy films until the 1960s and earned Rusholme the nickname of Manchester's Hollywood. Later the studios were used by the BBC.

An exhibition hall, measuring 600ft (182m) long × 216ft (66m) wide with a ground floor area of 100,000 square ft (30,300m²), was built on the corner of Whitworth Lane and Old Hall Lane in 1908. It was the second largest exhibition hall in England, but in 1913 it was burned down by suffragettes as a protest at a visit by Prime Minister Herbert Asquith.

The royal tour in Lancashire: their majesties acknowledging the salute of 25,000 children at Birch Fields, c.1912.

Novelist and playwright Ian Hay was born in 1876 at house named Platt Abbey in Rusholme; while cricket commentator, Neville Cardus, was born at Sumner Place in 1891, and learned to play cricket on the local Corporation rubbish tip.

☛ *See also* PLATT HALL; BIRCH HALL; NEVILLE CARDUS.

GLYNIS COOPER, THE ILLUSTRATED HISTORY OF THE MANCHESTER SUBURBS (2002); PETER HELM AND GAY SUSSEX, LOOKING BACK AT RUSHOLME AND FALLOWFIELD (1984).

RUTHERFORD, ERNEST (1871–1937)

A New Zealander who became a distinguished physicist and pioneered the study of atomic science. He was awarded a research scholarship in experimental physics at Cambridge University. Subsequently Rutherford discovered alpha rays and beta rays; and proved the possibility of splitting the atom. In 1907 he took up a post as Professor of Physics at Manchester University and lived at 17 Wilmslow Rd in Withington until 1919. He won the Nobel Prize for Chemistry in 1908 and in 1925 he was awarded the Order of Merit.

WWW.MANCHESTER2002-UK.COM

RYLANDS, JOHN (1801–1888)

'Manchester's most successful cotton magnate and one of the wealthiest self-made Englishmen of his day'. His merchanting warehouse was a plain white five-storey building on the corner of Piccadilly and Tib St. Today it houses Debenham's department store. John Rylands was married three times but had no surviving children. When he died in 1888 his widow, Enriqueta, built the John Rylands University Library on Deansgate as a tribute to him.

☛ *See also* JOHN RYLANDS UNIVERSITY LIBRARY.

WWW.MANCHESTER2002-UK.COM

S

S & J WATTS WAREHOUSE

Portland St. The best known of all Manchester's warehouses was designed in the 1850s by Travis and Mangall. The six-storey building had a different architectural style for each storey but each had a shared marine element in the design, presumably to reflect Watts's international trade with ships sailing all over the world. The interior followed the typical warehouse layout of the day. Sample rooms on the upper floors were reached by a central staircase; offices and the showroom were on the ground floor; and the packing department was in the basement. There were internal loading bays known as 'hovels' and wall cranes which were called 'teagles'. Watts's first premises were on Deansgate and were sold to Kendal Milne. Portland St was their fourth warehouse. James Watts was knighted by Queen Victoria and twice became Mayor of Manchester. Today the warehouse has been transformed into the upmarket Britannia Hotel.

GLYNIS COOPER, *HIDDEN MANCHESTER* (2004); SIMON TAYLOR ET AL., *MANCHESTER: THE WAREHOUSE LEGACY* (2002).

ST ANN'S CHURCH

St Ann's Square. The church was built by Lady Ann Bland and dedicated to St Ann, mother of the Virgin Mary, the name reflecting Lady Bland's own name and that of the reigning queen (1702–14). Building began in 1709 when Lady Ann laid the cornerstone in a large cornfield known as Acres

St Ann's Church, St Ann's Square.

Field where the harvest thanksgiving fair and the market were held. St Ann's was built of local red sandstone in the neoclassical style, typical features of which are round arched windows with Corinthian pilasters, a large round apse at the high altar end of the church, and galleries supported by Tuscan columns. The church was restored by Alfred Waterhouse in 1891. Originally the tower sported a wooden spire but this was removed in the 19th century after becoming structurally unsafe. The church tower is said to mark the exact centre of the City of Manchester and the OS arrow benchmark can be seen on the tower doorway.

The last interment in St Ann's graveyard took place on 31 May 1854. During the 1890s, as pressure increased for building land in the city centre, the gravestones were lowered to a foot (0.3m) below the pavement level, though the graves were left in situ, and the railings removed. John Shaw, who ran his punch house from what is now Sinclairs Oyster Bar, is buried here and a plaque on the north wall of the church tower gives instructions for locating his grave: 'his body lies five yards (4.5m) to the north and five feet (1.5m) to the west of the northwest corner of this tower'.

GLYNIS COOPER, *HIDDEN MANCHESTER* (2004); ST ANN'S CHURCH BROCHURE.

ST ANN'S SQUARE SHOPS

Partly built over the graveyard of St Ann's Church, the Royal Exchange is the main landmark. There are the exclusive Royal Exchange and Barton shopping arcades and other shops such as Aquascutum, Gap, Niketown and, appropriately, Past Times, to be sampled.

WWW.MANCHESTER2002-UK.COM

ST FRANCIS MONASTIC CHURCH, GORTON

St Francis Monastery Church has been described as the Taj Mahal of Manchester, despite its unlikely setting in downtown Gorton. In 1998 it was awarded World Heritage Status and it has been put on a list of the world's 100 most endangered sites (thanks to the local vandals); an unlikely stablemate of the Valley of the Kings and Pompeii.

The Franciscan Order of Brothers built the friary for their monastery next to the site of the church and then Edward Pugin designed their monastic church which took from 1866 to 1872 to build from red bricks with blue brick and stone dressings. The church was 184ft (56m) long, 98ft (29.6m) wide, and 100ft (30.3m) high and included a sanctuary, side chapels, a nave and aisles: 'pointed arched windows and rose windows … allow natural light to cascade throughout the church'. A pale green bell turret perched on top of a narrow steeple. Gifts of a stained-glass altar window, lady chapel, sanctuary lamp, wrought-iron communion railings, a font and a pulpit were gratefully received, and the church was finally completed in 1885 when the high altar, designed by Peter Paul Pugin and carved out of Bath stone, was installed. The whole site is now being restored under a regeneration scheme known as the Angels after the twelve statues of the saints rescued from the nave by Manchester City Council for safe storage until they could be returned to their rightful home.

WWW.GORTONMONASTERY.CO.UK

ST GEORGE'S CHURCH, HULME

St George's Church was built as the church for Hulme Barracks. The barracks were built in 1817, used by the cavalry until 1895 and then by the infantry until 1914 when most of the barracks were demolished. The church has survived but it is no longer a place of worship. Under a Hulme regeneration scheme in the 1990s the interior of the church was converted into flats, although the attractively Gothic ecclesiastical exterior of the building has been preserved.

GLYNIS COOPER, *HIDDEN MANCHESTER* (2004); CHRIS MAKEPEACE, *LOOKING BACK AT HULME, MOSS SIDE, CHORLTON-ON-MEDLOCK AND ARDWICK* (1998).

ST JAMES CHURCH, DIDSBURY

St James Church is built on the site of a wooden chapel which was 'of antiquity beyond memory' in 1235. In 1352 the chapel was given a consecrated graveyard to cope with the victims of the Black Death which had decimated Europe. The chapel was rebuilt in 1620 and a tower was added, giving it more the appearance of a church. St James was extended and rebuilt in 1842 and then further restored in 1855. During the earlier part of the 19th century a parsonage was built adjacent to the church but it acquired a reputation for being haunted. Clergymen of all denominations were hired to lay the unquiet spirits but nothing seemed to work and in 1850 it was abandoned. The church has remained in active use and today still lies at the heart of Didsbury village and its community life.

GLYNIS COOPER, *HISTORY OF THE MANCHESTER SUBURBS* (2002); T F WOODALL, *A NEW HISTORY OF DIDSBURY* (1976).

ST MARYS HOSPITAL

Established in 1790 on the corner of Hathersage Rd and Oxford Rd, it now specializes in maternity and gynaecology.

WWW.CMHT.NWEST.NHS.UK/HOSPITALS

ST NICHOLAS CHURCH

Kingsway, Burnage. Welch, Cachemaille-Day and Lander built this Anglican church in 1931–2 as a 'testament to the much overlooked art of brickwork'. The interior is white with tall narrow windows and a flat roof. Its German-inspired high curving walls create a very modern-looking design which Nikolaus Pevsner described as 'a milestone in the history of modern church architecture in England'; an accolade which earned the building Grade II listed status. The West Bay was added by Anthony Grimshaw in 1964.

WWW.MANCHESTER2002-UK.COM

SALFORD QUAYS

The Manchester Ship Canal, linking Cottonopolis with the open sea and thereby the outside world, was begun in 1887 and took seven years to complete. The canal was officially opened by Queen Victoria in 1894. The Manchester docks for the canal lay in three main units, mainly in neighbouring Salford. No. 9 Dock, the largest of the docks, was opened in 1905 by King Edward VII and Queen Alexandra.

Trade declined after the First World War and the docks finally closed in 1982. Since then a massive regeneration scheme has been responsible for cleaning the Ship Canal, stocking its waters with fish, and transforming the docks areas into a vibrant and upmarket complex of offices, shops, hotels, residential apartments, and a water sports centre.

☛ *See also* MANCHESTER SHIP CANAL.

WWW.THEQUAYS.ORG.UK; WWW.DESTINATIONSALFORD.COM

SAXON MANCHESTER

During the early 900s the Saxon King Alfred (of burnt cakes fame) and his son, Edward the Elder, wrested much of the power from the Danes and managed to reunite most of England. According to the Anglo-Saxon Chronicle, Edward took possession of Manchester in 923, repaired and garrisoned the town. St Mary's Church was founded around this time and the 'Angel Stone', most probably originally a likeness of the Archangel Michael, was placed in the new church. In 1028 King Canute founded one of his royal mints in Mamceastre.

☛ *See also* CATHEDRAL CHURCH OF ST MARY, ST DENYS AND ST GEORGE.

GLYNIS COOPER, *THE ILLUSTRATED HISTORY OF THE MANCHESTER SUBURBS* (2002).

SEDGWICK MILLS

Union St. 'U-shaped mill with 8 storeys and a 17 bay front opening onto Redhill Street', built by McConnell and Kennedy in 1819 and enlarged in 1860s.

ROBINA MCNEIL AND MICHAEL NEVELL, *A GUIDE TO THE INDUSTRIAL ARCHAEOLOGY OF GREATER MANCHESTER* (2000); MIKE WILLIAMS WITH D A FARNIE, *COTTON MILLS IN GREATER MANCHESTER* (1992).

SHAKESPEARE, THE

Fountain St. Although there has been an inn on this site since 1771, this charming black and white building, which dates from 1656, used to be the Shambles Inn at Chester and was removed to Manchester in 1928. It is said to be haunted by the ghost of a young girl who was raped by a chef there during the 19th century and subsequently died. The chef later hanged himself and the rope marks are said to be still visible on one of the beams. WWW.MANCHESTER2002-UK.COM

SHIPMAN, DR HAROLD (1946–2004)

Britain's most prolific mass murderer actually practised in Greater Manchester but he is indelibly associated with the city, much to its shame. Shipman studied medicine at Leeds before beginning work as a GP at Todmorden in Yorkshire. However he had become addicted to the painkiller, pethidine, and wrote his own prescriptions before injecting himself with the drug. When this was discovered he was sacked and heavily fined but, crucially, Shipman was not struck off the Medical Register. In 1977 he joined a medical practice at Hyde in the Greater Manchester borough of Tameside and 'Dr Death', as the press dubbed him, began his 'killing spree', which increased when he set up a practice on his own in 1993. His victims seemed to be mainly ladies of a certain age. Although concern was expressed about the high number of death certificates issued by him, nothing was done; and he was only caught when Kathleen Grundy, a former mayoress of Hyde, died unexpectedly and it was discovered that she had changed her will just two weeks beforehand, cutting out her three children and leaving £386,000 to Dr Shipman. Investigation revealed inconsistencies in other deaths and he was finally charged with fifteen murders. He was found guilty and sentenced to fifteen life sentences. A subsequent public inquiry conducted by Dame Janet Smith revealed that he probably killed at least 236 people. Harold Shipman committed suicide in January 2004 at Wakefield Prison; not out of remorse for his crimes or his victims, but, so it seems, to ensure that his wife would receive his pension. WWW.MANCHESTER2002-UK.COM

SHUDE HILL/WITHY GROVE

Two parts of the same street which runs from Corporation St up towards New Cross. The Printworks stands on the corner of Withy Grove and Corporation St, stretching back to Dantzig St.

SINCLAIRS OYSTER BAR

Off Exchange Square (formerly John Shaw's Punch House). The original building dates from the 14th century and used to stand next to the Old

Sinclairs Oyster Bar, formerly John Shaw's Punch House, with Molly Owen on the sign board.

Wellington Inn in the Old Shambles. It was removed once to make way for the Arndale development and again after the IRA bomb of 1996. In 1738 a man named John Shaw opened a punch house in the black and white timbered building. He served only punch in china bowls known as 'pees' and 'kews'. 'Pees' were larger and cost one shilling (£4.34 at 2002 values); 'kews' were smaller and cost six pence (£2.17 at 2002 values).Closing time was 8 pm sharp and those who overstayed their welcome were chased away by his housekeeper, Molly Owen, brandishing her mop and bucket and giving them a tongue lashing. It is Molly's portrait which is depicted on the sign board.

Oysters were first served at the former punch house in 1848 by the then landlord, Mr Wadsworth, who was a fishmonger. During the 1870s the inn was bought by Joseph Sinclair whose name it still bears. Oysters are still served today in a variety of dishes ranging from the traditional steak and oyster pie (wonderfully warming on a bitter winter's day) to Angels and Devils on Horseback.

GLYNIS COOPER, *HIDDEN MANCHESTER* (2003).

SIR HUGO OF CLAYTON HALL

This tragic legend dates back to the 12th century when Clayton Hall was owned by the de Buron or Byron family. Sir Hugo de Buron set on the Third Crusade leaving his beautiful young wife at the Hall. Time passed and Sir Hugo did not return and eventually someone told his wife that he had been killed in battle. She was completely devastated and died soon afterwards of a broken heart. Her funeral procession was met by a knight on his way home from the Crusades who turned out to be no other than Sir Hugo himself. Grief-stricken and full of remorse, he renounced his knighthood, surrendered his weapons and gave up fighting. Then, having made a full confession, he became a monk, taking his vows in the remote isolation of Kersal Cell high on Kersal Moor.

☛ *See also* CLAYTON.

GLYNIS COOPER, *THE ILLUSTRATED HISTORY OF THE MANCHESTER SUBURBS* (2002).

SLADE HALL

Slade Lane, Longsight/Levenshulme border. The Slade Estates were held by the Slade family from the 13th century but by 1584 the Siddalls from Withington had purchased all the lands. In 1585 Slade Hall was rebuilt by Edward and George Siddall and their initials together with the date are carved over the main doorway. The hall is a black and white timbered building with a framework of oak, 3 feet (0.9m) thick internal walls, rushes and plaster infill and square mullioned windows. It is a well-preserved building but today it is a private house.

Slade Hall on the Longsight/Levenshulme border.

GLYNIS COOPER, *THE ILLUSTRATED HISTORY OF THE MANCHESTER SUBURBS* (2002); GAY SUSSEX, *LONGSIGHT PAST AND PRESENT* (1982).

SLAVES, SUPPORT FOR

The American Civil War caused a cotton famine (1861–5) in Manchester. Mills shut down or went on to short working, causing severe hardship to thousands of Manchester cotton workers. The children who worked in the mills actually worked longer hours in far worse conditions than America's black slave children. Nevertheless, the Manchester cotton workers showed unswerving solidarity with their unpaid American counterparts. In 1862 an address was sent to Abraham Lincoln:

> the vast progress which you have made ... fills us with hope that every stain on your freedom will shortly be removed ... and the erasure of that foul blot on civilization and Christianity – chattel slavery ...

President Lincoln responded in a letter 'I know and deeply deplore the sufferings which the working people of Manchester ... are called to endure in this crisis'. When the Union, the Northern anti-slavery faction in America, finally won the war, a statue of Lincoln was erected to commemorate the support given by the workers of Manchester to the abolition of slavery. Extracts from Lincoln's letter adorn the plinth. The statue was originally erected in the grounds of Platt Hall but today it stands in Lincoln Square close to the Town Hall.

WWW.SPINNINGTHEWEB.ORG.UK

SMALL WARES

By the Tudor period Manchester had become well known for its 'small wares', which included ribbons, garters, braids, and laces for fastening clothes.

WWW.SPINNINGTHEWEB.ORG.UK

SPORTCITY

The City of Manchester Stadium is located in East Manchester on the Beswick/Clayton borders. It cost £90 million to build and can seat 38,000 people. Designed to provide a venue for the Commonwealth Games in 2002, the stadium has been the new home of Manchester City Football Club since 2003 and forms the centrepiece of an extensive sports complex known as Sportcity, which includes the National Cycling Centre, squash and table tennis centres.

WWW.MANCHESTER2002-UK.COM

SPORTS

Brief histories of Manchester United and Manchester City Football Clubs and Lancashire County Cricket Club are given separately. They grew from small local clubs to become the large concerns of today. During the latter part of the 19th century the management in mills and manufactories encouraged team sports and the formation of such clubs in the belief that it would help to foster team efforts in the workplace.

The number of different sports and sporting facilities around Manchester is now enormous and it is not possible to examine each one individually. Two facilities are of national importance: the Aquatics Centre, which is built to Olympic standards, and the Manchester Velodrome. A full list of what is available can be accessed via the cited website.

☛ *See also* LANCASHIRE COUNTY CRICKET CLUB; MANCHESTER CITY FOOTBALL CLUB; MANCHESTER UNITED FOOTBALL CLUB; MUNICH AIR DISASTER.

WWW.MANCHESTER2002-UK.COM

SPRING, HOWARD (D. 1965)

Although he was born in Cardiff, Howard Spring lived most of his life in Hesketh Avenue, Didsbury. The Olde Cock Inn in Didsbury featured in several of his novels. His best known works are *Fame is the Spur* and *My Son, My Son* (set in Ancoats), *Shabby Tiger* and *Rachel Rosling*.

WWW.MANCHESTER2002-UK.COM

STOCKPORT ROAD CORRIDOR INITIATIVE

Regeneration and improvement of Ardwick, Longsight and Levenshulme; and cleaning up the railway lands.

ALAN KIDD, *HISTORY OF MANCHESTER* (3RD EDN, 2002); WWW.MANCHESTER 2002-UK.COM

STOPES, MARIE (1880–1958)

She was born in Surrey but studied for a degree in botany and zoology at Manchester University, and then a doctorate which she completed in Munich. She became the first female science lecturer at Manchester University, lecturing on fossil plants and coal mining. She married Dr Reginald Gates but the marriage was annulled in 1916 on the grounds of non-consummation. Marie Stopes was appalled at her own ignorance of sexual love, in common with many women of her generation, and decided to educate herself in the matter through reading books in the British Museum. In 1917 she married Manchester aircraft manufacturer, Humphrey Verdon Roe (1878–1949), and wrote her best-selling *Married Love* in 1918. Marie Stopes pioneered birth control clinics in England and opened her first clinic in 1921. The clinics were free and aimed largely at poor women to prevent them being burdened with large families. The reaction from men was furious. She was verbally abused, spat at and threatened for 'interfering with their virility'. It was believed by many men that large families 'proved they were men', provided potential wage earners, and of course repeated pregnancies were an excellent way of keeping their wives under control. More than one man killed his wife when her child-bearing days were over, claiming that 'freedom from pregnancy had caused her to go wild'. Marie Stopes was not deterred and it is to her courage and perseverance that the young women of the 21st century owe a debt for their freedom to choose when and how they have their families.

CHAMBERS BIOGRAPHICAL DICTIONARY.

STRANGEWAYS HALL

Cheetham Hill. Strangeways Hall stood in its own park on the edge of Cheetham looking out over the suburb. It was the seat of the Strangeways family but by 1770 it had become home to Lord Ducie. By 1860 the Hall was unoccupied and it was demolished in 1863. The new Assize Courts, designed by Alfred Waterhouse, were built on the site and opened in 1864. Strangeways Prison was built behind the courts and opened in 1868. GLYNIS COOPER, *THE ILLUSTRATED HISTORY OF THE MANCHESTER SUBURBS* (2002).

STRANGEWAYS PRISON
Cheetham. Designed in 1861 by Alfred Waterhouse after he made visits to Reading Gaol and Holloway Prison. The circular concept was suggested by Joshua Jebb, Surveyor General of Prisons, who designed Pentonville in the 1840s. Strangeways Prison was built of red brick on the site of Strangeways Park, with a tower like 'a medieval Italian campanile (bell tower)', to hold 1,000 prisoners, and opened in 1869. Christabel Pankhurst was briefly incarcerated here in October 1906.
WWW.MANCHESTER2002-UK.COM

SUNLIGHT, JOE (1890–1979)
Joe Sunlight was born in Russia to a Jewish family but they fled to England when he was 12 and settled in Manchester. He trained in architecture and spent his life working in Manchester. He was kept busy and in Prestwich alone he designed over 1,000 houses. His greatest distinction was to be the architect of Manchester's first high-rise office block. Sunlight House on Quay St was fourteen storeys high and was Manchester's tallest building when it was erected during the 1930s. It had high-speed lifts and a 'unique vacuum cleaning system ... to keep its 3000 windows dust free'. Joe Sunlight enjoyed horse racing and owned racehorses as well. In later life he became an MP for the Liberal Party.
WWW.MANCHESTER2002-UK.COM

SWIVEL HOUSE
This is a tale that Fletcher Moss researched in Didsbury but was refused permission to publish. The house concerned was renamed several times and eventually rebuilt and finally he published his story but gave no identifying details.

> ... each night at about midnight a lady would appear in one of the bedrooms dressed in frills and furbelows, powders and pattens, and a gown of green brocade rustling like autumn leaves ... she lingered by the foot of the bed for a few moments before silently fading into the wall. Legend rumoured that she was the sweetheart of a previous owner who had been a very wealthy man and that she had been walled up alive because she knew too much about how he had come by his wealth. During 19th

century alterations to the house 'a secret chamber' was discovered in the chimney stack containing the decaying remains of an old chair and table, and chicken bones.

☛ *See also* DIDSBURY HAUNTS.
THE WRITINGS OF FLETCHER MOSS ARE HELD BY CENTRAL LIBRARY IN ST PETER'S SQUARE MANCHESTER.

T

TAYLOR, WILLIAM HORACE (1908–1999)
He was born in Manchester and attended Manchester Grammar School. After leaving school he worked at the Manchester Docks and then joined the Admiralty in 1939. During the Second World War he was a bomb disposal engineer and won the George Cross for the disabling and disposing of mines in September and October 1940.
WWW.MANCHESTER2002-UK.COM

THAW, JOHN (1942-2002)
Actor, born in Longsight. His father was a lorry driver and the family lived in Burnage. He worked as a potato porter in Manchester's Smithfield market before studying at RADA. His first experience of acting was as an amateur in Burnage but he was best known for his television roles in *Inspector Morse* and *The Sweeney*. He married the well-known actress Sheila Hancock.
WWW.MANCHESTER2002-UK.COM

TIB STREET
This runs from Swan St to Market St. The culverted River Tib, which hasn't seen daylight for 200 years, runs below the street, giving it its name. It lies in the bohemian Northern Quarter and was once famous for pet shops. Afflecks Palace is on corner of Tib St and Church St.

Holland Hydroponics, Tib St. Tib St used to be full of pet shops.

Tib St Horn by David Kemp, corner of Tib St and Church St in the Northern Quarter, 2003.

TOWN HALL

Albert Square. Completed in 1887, this neo-Gothic building, inspired by 13th-century architecture and designed by Alfred Waterhouse, soars 286 feet above Manchester, reflecting the civic dignity of city status, achieved in 1853. Internally it is a symphony of hammerbeam ceilings, lavish civic rooms, mosaic floors decorated with the 'busy bees' which were a symbol of Manchester's hive of industry in the 19th century, murals and a maze of dark

Main entrance to Manchester Town Hall in Albert Square.

vaulted corridors, endless staircases, offices and tiny hidden rooms. The Great Hall is designed in the style of a Flemish weaving hall, a tribute to the 14th-century Flemish weavers who settled in Manchester at the invitation of Edward III and on whose skills the basis of the Manchester textile industry was founded. Twelve murals by Ford Madox Ford adorn the walls. Three great spiral staircases sweep upwards from the entrance hall with its innumerable busts and statues of the city forefathers. A statue of the Roman governor, Agricola, stands over the main entrance, in tribute to the fact that he established the first 'Mamceastre' almost 2,000 years ago. Around the external wall are statues of those who have played an important part in the development of the city. The Town Hall faces and dominates Albert Square, with its large ornate monument (designed by Thomas Worthington) to Queen Victoria's consort at its centre eternally staring at the Town Hall. No doubt he would have approved of the style of this status symbol. The square is used as a venue for celebrations and street fairs, BBC roadshows, outside broadcasts, Christmas markets (like St Ann's Square) and as a focal point for festive gatherings such as the Irish Festival in March or the Chinese New Year.

MANCHESTER.VISITOR.CENTRE@NOTES.MANCHESTER.GOV.UK

Town Hall.

TOWN HALL EXTENSION

Designed by Vincent Harris, who designed the neighbouring Central Library, this eight-storey building was built in 1937 to accommodate expanding municipal departments which dealt with rates, rents, gas, electricity, street cleaning, etc. and to provide a large council chamber. The southern wall of the building was curved to match the library's circular design and separated from it by Library Walk. The Extension was built in Gothic style of stone from Darley Dale, with stained-glass windows by George Gray representing the Lancastrian coat of arms, and it was opened by King George VI in 1938. The Extension is linked by two covered walkways to the Town Hall at first floor level in Lloyd St. The building also houses the Tourist Information and Visitor Centre which is at ground floor level facing St Peter's Square.

MANCHESTER.VISITOR.CENTRE@NOTES.MANCHESTER.GOV.UK

TRIANGLE, THE

Exchange Square/Corner of Hanging Ditch/ Corporation St. The triangular building of the former Corn Exchange was built near the site of a corn mill which had stood on the banks of the Irk. During building work in the early 19th century on Cateaton St, which runs from Hanging Ditch to Victoria St/Deansgate, 'a bed or mass of shudes or shells of oats, quite black – there were cartloads of these shudes' were discovered at a depth of several feet. Shude Hill runs north-east away from the Corn Exchange towards the probable site of another corn mill. Two water-driven corn mills were recorded in the area in 1282.

In 1903 the new Corn and Produce Exchange was designed to reflect Manchester's growing importance. It was about six storeys high and had a large ground floor hall with innumerable tiered side offices dominated by a central glass dome. The green and white tiled entrance has been preserved together with dizzying flights of stairs around a central stairwell. Foodstuffs and raw materials were traded here for over half a century; but times changed and by the 1980s/1990s the Corn Exchange had become an 'alternative shopping market' with vegetarian foods, New Age shops, music, clothing, palmists, tarot readers, aromatherapy products, etc. After the damage caused by the IRA bomb in 1996 the old Corn Exchange was restored, refurbished and renamed The Triangle and it is now an upmarket shopping centre specializing in designer labels, body care products and coffee shops.

J Reilly, *History of Manchester* (c.1880–9); Glynis Cooper, *Hidden Manchester* (2004).

The Triangle, formerly the Corn and Produce Exchange. A corn mill used to stand near this spot.

TUDOR/STUART MANCHESTER

Manchester was described by John Leland, *c.*1536, as 'the fairest, the best buildid, quikkest and most populous tounne of all Lancastreshire'. The town was already renowned for its 'small wares' (ribbons, garters, laces, braids) and in 1552 an Act was passed to regulate the quality of 'Manchester cottons' (a napped woollen weave material).

During the 17th century Manchester was the only Parliamentarian stronghold in the North-West and a statue of Oliver Cromwell which stood near the Cathedral commemorated this fact.

ALAN KIDD, *HISTORY OF MANCHESTER* (3RD EDN, 2002).

TURPIN, DICK (1704–1737)

The notorious highwayman, Dick Turpin, spent the last few years of his life in the 1730s living near Brough in Yorkshire. He was fond of drinking and gambling and he was a frequent visitor to the Manchester Races which were held on Kersal Moor. There were several reports in the newspapers of the time that he attended the races with his married girlfriend who dressed as a boy to avoid recognition. Turpin frequented the Broughton and Cheetham localities of Manchester but there are many pubs in the Manchester area with a Dick Turpin tradition.

CHAMBERS BIOGRAPHICAL DICTIONARY.

U

UMIST (UNIVERSITY OF MANCHESTER INSTITUTE OF SCIENCE AND TECHNOLOGY)

UMIST was founded as a Mechanics Institute in 1824 at the Bridgewater Arms on Tib St. Sponsored by local employers and bankers, the Institute offered courses in scientific and technical subjects but also grammar, writing and arithmetic, so that clerks, warehousemen and shopkeepers soon outnumbered mechanics. The first UMIST buildings stood on Sackville St and opened in 1892 as the Manchester Municipal Technical School. Under the Technical Instruction Act of 1899 the school began to evolve into UMIST after 1902 and it became the first UK university to offer degrees in chemical engineering.

WWW.UMIST.AC.UK

School of Technology.

UNIVERSITY OF MANCHESTER
☞ *See* VICTORIA UNIVERSITY OF MANCHESTER.

URBIS
Cathedral Gardens. Urbis is a very modern concept, a vision in glass somehow reminiscent of the now retired Concorde aeroplane, which proclaims itself to be a museum of urban life. It is therefore not just about Manchester, but about other large cities the world over, including Los Angeles, Paris, Sao Paulo, Singapore and Tokyo. Interactive exhibitions involve visitors and focus on the present as much as on the past. A 'funicular

Urbis urban museum and the Printworks.

glass elevator', inspired surely by the lifts of the Eiffel Tower, gives access to four exhibition levels.

WWW.MANCHESTER2002-UK.COM

V

VERDON-ROE, SIR EDWIN ALLIOT (1877–1958)

Born in Patricroft in Manchester in 1877, he became a celebrated aircraft designer after serving as an apprentice with the Lancashire and Yorkshire Railways and studying marine engineering at King's College, London. In 1899 Roe worked for the British & South African Royal Mail Company as an engineer and won a prize of £75 for a design of a model flying machine in 1907. With the prize money he built a full-size aeroplane based on his winning model. The first test flight was abortive but in 1908, fitted with a more powerful engine, Roe succeeded in getting the plane airborne and making several short flights – the first British-built plane to fly under its own power.

He founded the AVRO company (based on his own name and initials) with his brother Edwin in Manchester in 1910, and in Oldham built the famous AVRO 504 biplane in 1913, the most commonly used military aircraft in the First World War. The Armstrong Siddeley Company took over AVRO in 1928.

WWW.MANCHESTER2002-UK.COM

VICTORIA MILLS

Varley St, Miles Platting. Designed and built by architect George Woodhouse for William Holland, two identical six-storey mills built in 1867 and 1873 and linked by a common engine house with an octagonal chimney. The mill was working until 1960 and then became derelict until it was refurbished as luxury apartments and a community centre, but retaining the original features, under a regeneration scheme during the late 20th century.

ROBINA MCNEIL AND MICHAEL NEVELL, *A GUIDE TO THE INDUSTRIAL ARCHAEOLOGY OF GREATER MANCHESTER* (2000); MIKE WILLIAMS WITH D A FARNIE, *COTTON MILLS IN GREATER MANCHESTER* (1992).

VICTORIA PARK

Not an original settlement or suburb, this grew out of an exclusive housing development built in the 1840s on the edge of Rusholme and named after the new and popular queen. There were to be three main crescents of houses designed by architect Richard Lane, but only two of the crescents were ever built. Eminent inhabitants included the distinguished chemist Sir Henry Roscoe, Richard Cobden and John Bright, who helped to found the Anti Corn Law League, the artist Ford Madox Brown, conductor and musician Sir Charles Halle, George Hadfield MP, and the suffragette Emmeline Pankhurst. Benjamin Disraeli stayed at Ashburne House, which eventually became a hall of residence for students at Manchester University, as did most of the other large old houses in Victoria Park.

GLYNIS COOPER, *THE ILLUSTRATED HISTORY OF THE MANCHESTER SUBURBS* (2002); E A BOSDIN LEECH, *A SHORT ACCOUNT OF VICTORIA PARK, MANCHESTER* (1937).

VICTORIA STATION

Hunts Bank. The original station was quite small and had just a single platform. It opened in 1842 to serve the Manchester and Leeds Railway which ran trans-Pennine services to Harrogate, Leeds, York and Bradford. By the 1880s however the station had grown and dominated Long Millgate, its

Victoria Station, Manchester, c.1910.

iron and glass canopy, 160 yards (145m) long, proudly proclaiming that trains for Leeds, Harrogate, Bradford, York, Scarborough, Newcastle, Hull, Belgium, Liverpool, Southport, Blackpool, Fleetwood, Goole, Ireland, Scotland and London, would depart from the station, although today it mainly serves stations to the north and east of Manchester. The 700ft (212m) engine sheds, built by George Stephenson, have survived to the present day. ALAN KIDD, *HISTORY OF MANCHESTER* (3RD EDN, 2002); WWW.MANCHESTER 2002-UK.COM

VICTORIA UNIVERSITY OF MANCHESTER
Oxford Rd. The university began life in 1851 as Owens College, which was situated in Richard Cobden's former house on Quay St. The college moved to Oxford Rd in 1873 into buildings designed by Alfred Waterhouse on the site of the house where Crompton Potter, the uncle of Beatrix Potter, was born. In 1902 Whitworth College was built adjacent to Owens College and the following year both institutions became the Victoria University of Manchester. A School of Medicine is also attached to the University. WWW.MAN.AC.UK

Owens College, c.1902, before it became the Victoria University.

VILLAGE, THE

An area at the heart of the former 'warehouse city' of Cottonopolis, which includes clubs, pubs and various other facilities for gay and lesbian people, the Gay Village is centred around the cafe society of Chorlton St and Canal St, not far from Piccadilly Gardens; and extends as far as Dale St, Sackville St, Whitworth St and Princess St, close to China Town. In 1992, 'Queer Up North', the country's first gay arts festival, took place. The Festival brings UK and international artists from the worlds of contemporary dance, theatre, music, comedy, cabaret, etc. to Manchester every May/June.
WWW.MANCHESTER2002-UK.COM

VIMTO MONUMENT

Granby Row. A larger than life-size burnished wooden model of a bottle of Vimto, surrounded by the raspberries, blackcurrants and herbs used in its manufacture, was designed by sculptor Kerry Morrison in 1992. The monument stands on Granby Row, near Piccadilly Station, on the site of the premises where Vimto was first created from a secret recipe by John Nicholls in 1908. It was advertised as a herbal tonic which would give drinkers 'vim and vigour', hence the name. Today the company is based in Salford and run by the grandsons of John Nicholls.
GLYNIS COOPER, *HIDDEN MANCHESTER* (2004).

W

WAKES WEEKS

The wakes holiday developed out of the holy days celebrated by the church, but people also celebrated other high days, important in the agricultural calendar, such as May Day, Midsummer, Harvest Home (Lughnasa). Originally, 'wakes' was a

A light dusting of snow lies on the Vimto Monument marking the site of 49 Granby Row where Vimto was first produced to a secret recipe in 1908.

religious festival held to celebrate the day of the patron saint of the local church; so to each congregation their saint's day was viewed as the most important day of the year. The name 'Wake' comes from the practice of staying awake all night to pray, on the eve of a saint's day. The term 'funeral wake' is from the same origin. By the 1800s the wakes had become a time of merrymaking, with fairs and dancing, eating and drinking to excess, but for the factory workers in the early 1800s, these celebrations were out of reach. Long hours and bad working conditions meant that wakes were just a childhood memory for most of them. However, by 1870 the idea of a week's holiday for factory workers, albeit unpaid, was beginning to be accepted. As it was more cost effective for the mill to shut down completely and give everyone a week off, it became usual for all the mills in one area to close together. Reviving the old name for celebrations this became 'Wakes Week'.
WWW.SPINNINGTHEWEB.ORG.UK

WARNER, DAVID (B. 1941)
Manchester-born David Warner trained at RADA and made his name with the RSC. He is best known for his portrayal of an eccentric Marxist in *Morgan – a Suitable Case for Treatment*. He has also appeared in a number of other films including *Straw Dogs* and *The Bofors Gun*.
WWW.MANCHESTER2002-UK.COM

WATERHOUSE, ALFRED (1830–1905)
Although he was born in Liverpool and educated in London, Alfred Waterhouse set up an architectural practice in Manchester and did some of his best creative work there. He studied in France, Italy and Germany, and the influence of the architecture of these countries can be seen in his work. He was responsible for designing the Town Hall on Albert Square in 1877; the new Owens College when it moved to Oxford Rd in 1873; Manchester Museum on Oxford Rd; the Refuge Assurance Building on Oxford St; and Strangeways Prison on the edge of Cheetham Hill. He also designed his own house in Fallowfield but unfortunately it has not survived. Nationally he is best known for designing the Natural History Museum in South Kensington. Alfred Waterhouse was President of the Royal Institute of British Architects (1888–91) and by way of keeping it in the family, his son, Paul, and grandson, Michael, have held the same post in turn.
WWW.MANCHESTER2002-UK.COM; *CHAMBERS BIOGRAPHICAL DICTIONARY.*

WHALLEY, JOANNE (B. 1964)
Born in Manchester, she became a versatile stage and screen actress. She played Christine Keeler in *Scandal*, the story of the John Profumo affair which brought down Harold Macmillan's government, and has appeared in films

including *The Singing Detective, Dance with a Stranger* and *Kill Me Again*. She married the American actor Val Kilmer and was known as Joanne Whalley-Kilmer until her divorce, when she reverted to use of her stage name taken from a Manchester suburb.
WWW.MANCHESTER2002-UK.COM

WHALLEY RANGE

This suburb is comparatively recent and is probably best known because Salford actress, Joanne Whalley, took her stage surname from it. The area was originally known as Jackson's Moss but when Samuel Brooks built up the Moss during the latter part of the 19th century he renamed it with what he imagined to be the classier sounding name of Whalley Range. Whalley is an old Lancashire word for a clearing alongside a road and range can mean an enclosure. Brooks's home, Whalley House, lay on Whalley Rd. The Whalley Hotel was built on the site of Oak Cottage farm at Brooks' Bar (the former toll gate). Nearby was a pond where thatching straw was washed before use and in which fruit and vegetables were cleaned before being sent to market.

William Hulme's Grammar School, one of a series founded in the North-West by that gentleman (d. 1691), stands on Spring Bridge Rd. The school was for boys only; but today girls are equally well catered for by Whalley Range High School for Girls which opened in 1891 and stands on Wilbraham Rd opposite the playing fields of the boys' school.

Like Longsight, there is great religious diversity in Whalley Range. Apart from mosques and Islamic centres of worship, there is the Manchester Chinese Church, the Manchester Pioneer Centre for Spiritualism, St Edmund's Roman Catholic Church and the Cenacle Church of England.
GLYNIS COOPER, THE ILLUSTRATED HISTORY OF THE MANCHESTER SUBURBS (2002).

WHIT WALKS AND WHIT WEEK

One popular celebration was the Whit Walks, or Processions of Witness, inaugurated in Manchester in 1801. Most people would buy, or make, new clothes especially for the day, thus helping the commerce of the town. The girls dressed in their new white cotton dresses, the boys in crisp white shirts or even all-white sailor suits, would meet up at the local school or church and in smart white lines they would follow the banner. At the head of the procession a band led the way around the parish, until they would end up back at the starting point for tea and buns followed by an afternoon of fun and games. Whit Walks continued in Manchester until the 1960s.

By the last quarter of the 19th century Whit Sunday and Whit Monday had replaced Whit Friday as the day the walks were held. Gradually the festivities stretched into a week. Typically, the Church of England would hold a walk on Whit Monday; other denominations would hold walks on the Tuesday; on Wednesday there would be games and tea for children at a farm or community hall; on Thursday there would be a local outing; and on Friday there would be a daytrip further afield.

There were also Whitsun Ales, which themselves were not a form of alcohol, but country fairs. The fairs featured Morris dancing, music, sports and general merrymaking. There is a surviving description by Blount in 1679 of a Whitsun Ale, known as the Kirklington Lamb Ale:

> the custom is, that on Monday after Whitsun week, there is a fat live lamb provided, and the maids of the town, having their thumbs tied behind them, run after it, and she that with her mouth takes and hold the lamb is declared 'Lady of the Lamb' ... attended with music and a Morisco dance of men, and another of women, where the rest of the day is spent in dancing, mirth and merry glee.

WWW.SPINNINGTHEWEB.ORG.UK

WHITWORTH, SIR JOSEPH (1803–1887)
Born in Stockport he was a philanthropist and engineer, whose name is commemorated in Manchester in street names, an art gallery and a park. His first workshop was in Chorlton St, Manchester, a forerunner of the Whitworth Works in Openshaw. Whitworth specialized in cotton manufacturing machinery but he is best known for his standardized screw threads. He lived in Fallowfield and helped found the Manchester School of Design.
CHAMBERS BIOGRAPHICAL DICTIONARY.

WILCOX, PAULA (B. 1949)
Manchester-born Paula Wilcox attended the Hollies Grammar School in West Didsbury and studied at the National Youth Theatre. She has worked on stage, screen and in the West End but she is best known for her roles in *The Lovers* opposite the late Richard Beckinsale and in *Man About the House* with Richard O'Sullivan.
WWW.MANCHESTER2002-UK.COM

WILKINSON, ELLEN (1901–1947)
Ellen Wilkinson was born in Coral St, Ardwick, the only child of Methodist parents. She was educated at Ardwick School and Manchester University, all paid for through scholarships which she won. For a while she taught at the Oswald Rd Elementary School. At 16 she became passionately interested in socialism and the aims of the suffragettes. In 1915 Ellen became an official for the Union of Distributive and Allied Workers and in 1924, already a

member of Manchester City Council, she was elected MP for Middlesborough East. She became known in the House of Commons as Red Ellen due to both the colour of her hair and her politics. After opposing Ramsay MacDonald when he was elected in 1929, she lost her seat in 1931 and spent a few years writing political books and a novel.

In 1935 she became MP for Jarrow, where nearly 80 per cent of the population was unemployed, and in 1936 she organized and led the famous Jarrow Hunger March to London. Ellen was an active MP and later in 1936 she travelled to Spain to support the International Brigades in their fight against the fascist Franco. The following year she pushed reforms through Parliament, which became law in 1938, requiring traders to state how much interest was to be paid on goods bought under hire purchase.

Ellen was appointed Parliamentary Secretary to the Ministry of Pensions in Winston Churchill's Coalition Government of 1940; and in 1945 she was appointed Minister of Education by Clement Attlee, becoming the first woman to hold this post. She failed in her ambition to have the school-leaving age raised to 16 but in 1946 she oversaw the passing of the School Milk Act which provided free milk to all schoolchildren. Depressed by what she saw as her failure to achieve all of her reforms, she died of an overdose of barbiturates in February 1947. Nicholls Hospital, a boy's school built in 1881 on Hyde Rd, was renamed the Ellen Wilkinson School in her memory.
WWW.SPARTACUS.SCHOOLNET.CO.UK

WITHINGTON

In Domesday Book Withington and Ladybarn were declared 'waste'; that there were no farms, no swine, no honey and no mill. Withington was first recorded in 1186 as having a farm in a willow copse. A withy is a branch of willow used for binding bundles. By 1200, however, the manor of Withington was extensive and included Didsbury, Burnage, Chorlton-cum-Hardy, Rusholme, Fallowfield, Moss Side, Levenshulme, plus Denton and Haughton, both in Tameside, a district of Greater Manchester.

The suburb remained rural until the 20th century when Corporation housing estates were built on a large scale, with 10,000 homes on the site of Old Hall Farm, a former moated manor house, and many more besides on other developments such as Albert Park. In 1871 nearly twelve times as many people in Withington were 'in service' to the local gentry as worked in the cotton mills.

There is a story that one day in 1886 a cow and a flock of sheep were being driven through Withington when the cow, wanting some diversion, decided to go shopping. The creature entered a number of local shops but the drover excused the animal's behaviour by saying that walking with sheep was beneath the dignity of your average cow and had caused it so much shame that the cow had been obliged to protest!

Today Withington is best known for its hospitals which include the internationally renowned Christies Hospital, dedicated to the care of cancer patients, and the Holt Radium Institute, which has developed pioneering work in the treatment of cancer.

GLYNIS COOPER, THE ILLUSTRATED HISTORY OF THE MANCHESTER SUBURBS (2002); KENNETH WHITTAKER, A HISTORY OF WITHINGTON (1957).

WITHINGTON HOSPITAL

The forerunner of this hospital was Chorlton Union Workhouse built on Nell Lane in 1854. It was extended by the addition of 'pavilions' across the road in 1864, designed by Thomas Worthington and approved by Florence Nightingale. On what is now the car park there was a 'tented hospital' set up in 1917 to deal with military casualties from the First World War.

☛ *See also* THOMAS WORTHINGTON.

WWW.CMHT.NWEST.NHS.UK/HOSPITALS

WOOD, MICHAEL (B. 1948)

A historian, writer, film maker, broadcaster, musician and excellent story teller, Michael Wood was born in Chorlton-on-Medlock, one of the inner Manchester suburbs. He was educated at Manchester Grammar School and Oriel College, Oxford; but though he now lives in London he has never forgotten his northern roots. Some of his best known television series include: *In Search of the Dark Ages, Domesday, In the Footsteps of Alexander the Great, In Search of the Trojan War, Legacy, In Search of Shakespeare, Conquistadors, In Search of Myths and Heroes.*

WWW.MANCHESTER2002-UK.COM

WOOLWORTH'S FIRES

Two disastrous fires occurred in the late 20th century at Woolworth's store in Piccadilly. The first, in which ten people died and forty-seven were hurt, broke out in May 1979. The deaths were largely as a result of toxic fumes from foam. Less than ten years later eleven people died in 1988 when fire broke out in the upper storeys and it was found that the emergency exits were locked. Woolworth's no longer have a store on Piccadilly.

WWW.MANCHESTERONLINE.CO.UK

New fountains in Piccadilly Gardens. The building in the background is the former Woolworth's store.

WORTHINGTON, THOMAS (1826–1909)

He was born in The Crescent in Salford and was apprenticed to architects Bowman and Crowther when he was 14. By the time he was 18 he had won a Society of Arts Gold Medal for one of his designs. He spent some time in Italy studying its architecture with Sir William Tate. Worthington was a Unitarian and he had a strong social conscience. After he set up his own business in Manchester he sought 'social commissions', designing Salford Baths and Laundries (1857) and Chorlton Union Hospital 'pavilions' (1864); the City Police and Sessions Court on Minshull St (1868); and several Unitarian chapels. Worthington is best known, however, for designing the Albert Memorial on Albert Square (1862).

WWW.MANCHESTER2002-UK.COM

WYTHENSHAWE

The suburb takes its name from a willow wood which once belonged to Wythenshawe Hall when it was the seat of the Tatton family. Until the 1920s Wythenshawe was little more than a collection of ancient halls and small farms. Then Barry Parker, architect and follower of William Morris, followed his dream and created a new garden city. Today Corporation housing estates have swelled the population to over 100,000, roughly the size of a city like Cambridge.

Wythenshawe Hall, a beautiful former moated black and white timbered Tudor manor house, has survived, standing incongruously among modern bricks and concrete. Not far away, Baguley Hall, built in 1320, and boasting some fine 14th-century groining and trefoil work, has also managed to survive the ravages of modern times.

Manchester Airport lies on the Wythenshawe boundaries. It was the first municipal airport in the country, which saw Amy Johnson land her biplane on the tarmac shortly before her last flight when she disappeared without trace. The first man in space, Yuri Gagarin, landed at Manchester Airport in 1961; and the first jumbo landed there in 1970, followed by Concorde in 1971. Today the airport handles over twelve million passengers a year.

☛ *See also* WYTHENSHAWE HALL.

GLYNIS COOPER, *ILLUSTRATED HISTORY OF THE MANCHESTER SUBURBS* (2002); *WYTHENSHAWE: THE STORY OF A GARDEN CITY* (DERRICK DEAKIN, 1989)

WYTHENSHAWE HALL

Wythenshawe. The Hall was the seat of the Tatton family. It was built as a moated manor house in Tudor times by Robert Tatton and is a fine black and white timbered building with multi gables. Today it used as a conference hall and an art gallery and it is licensed for weddings. Wythenshawe Park in its grounds was gifted to the City of Manchester by Ernest and Sheena Simon. There is a community farm which sells home-reared beef, lamb and pork. Herbs, fruit and alpine plants are also grown as well as a more exotic collection of bananas, pineapples, tea, coffee and rice on the Safari Walk.

There was a chapel in the grounds of the Hall until 1688 but nothing of it remains today. A statue of Oliver Cromwell in the park formerly stood near Manchester Cathedral and commemorated the fact that Manchester was the only Parliamentarian stronghold in the North-West during the Civil War. In November 1642 the hall was besieged by the Roundheads and six Royalist supporters lost their lives. One of them was engaged to a local girl named Mary Webb. Unable to accept her loss she spent two months tracking down Captain Adams, who had led the siege, and shot him dead at point blank

range with a rifle. She made no attempt to escape. All she had wanted was justice for her dead sweetheart.
GLYNIS COOPER, THE ILLUSTRATED HISTORY OF THE MANCHESTER SUBURBS (2002); WWW.MANCHESTER2003-UK.COM

Y

YE OLD COCK INN
Didsbury. The pub stands adjacent to the 'Gates of Hell' of Didsbury parsonage. The inn formerly had a cockpit where fowls fought to the death and much money was made in betting on the outcome. Today the cockpit has gone and the inn in this picturesque and olde worlde part of Didsbury is very popular with students in the summer months. The Cock Inn shares a large grassed area, once part of the former cobbled roadway, with the neighbouring Didsbury Hotel. St James Church standing in the background gives the whole place very much the air of a village green.
GLYNIS COOPER, THE ILLUSTRATED HISTORY OF THE MANCHESTER SUBURBS (2002); T F WOODALL, A NEW HISTORY OF DIDSBURY (1976).

YE OLD SEVEN STARS
Shude Hill. This black and white timbered inn no longer exists, but in a copy of *Manchester Notes and Queries* dating from the end of the 19th century there is a short piece about Ye Old Seven Stars:

> there is an old inn, or tavern, at the foot of Shude Hill in Manchester, called the Seven Stars, which, it is said, has been a licensed house since AD 1350; the proof of which lies in Lancaster Castle, where are deposited the records of the various licenses.

The Manchester City News for 25 April 1885 also mentions the inn:

> in the course of structural alterations which were being carried on at the Seven Stars Hotel, Withy Grove, Manchester, some discoveries of silver plate were made, which pointed to the conclusion that, during the Cromwellian era, that house was occupied by the troops of Charles I, and that a then celebrated regiment of dragoons had occasion to secrete their mess plate there, in some case of emergency ...

WWW.GMCRO.CO.UK; LANCASHIRE RECORD OFFICE, NEWSPAPER CUTTINGS OF MANCHESTER AND SALFORD (c.1908).

The Seven Stars Hotel in Shude Hill said to have been licensed in 1350. Guy Fawkes was rumoured to have stayed here.